P9-EEF-590

Editor
Mara Ellen Guckian

Editorial Project Manager
Ina Massler Levin, M.A.

Editor-in-Chief
Sharon Coan, M.S. Ed.

Illustrator
Renée Christine Yates

Cover Artist
Lesley Palmer

Art Coordinator
Kevin Barnes

Art Manager
CJae Froshay

Imaging
James Edward Grace
Rosa C. See

Product Manager
Phil Garcia

Publisher
Mary D. Smith, M.S. Ed.

U.S. History Little Books
FAMOUS EVENTS

Authors
Brenda Strickland, M.S. and Pat Terrell Walker, M.A.

Teacher Created Resources

Teacher Created Resources, Inc.
6421 Industry Way
Westminster, CA 92683
www.teachercreated.com
ISBN: 978-0-7439-3258-5
©2002 Teacher Created Resources, Inc.
Reprinted, 2008
Made in U.S.A.

The classroom teacher may reproduce copies of materials in this book for classroom use only. The reproduction of any part for an entire school or school system is strictly prohibited. No part of this publication may be transmitted, stored, or recorded in any form without written permission from the publisher.

Table of Contents

Introduction

State requirements have become increasingly specific concerning the subject matter educators are expected to teach. Teachers have found it more and more difficult to find curriculum materials to meet students' needs. Teachers need age-appropriate history materials. Many teachers are searching local libraries and the Web. Often, the materials and information found are too advanced for the primary level.

The *U.S. History Little Books* series provides young children with simple, fact-filled books that they can make. The Little Books focus on important people, places, and events in United States history. Maps of the area being discussed are included for each Little Book topic. A map of the United States is also included on each map page to give students a point of reference. Another reference tool, the time line (pages 8–10), can be enlarged and displayed in the classroom.

Research indicates that children retain more information when they are personally involved in the learning process. Hands-on activities guarantee involvement. Children will have fun creating folded books, layered books, pop-up books, and lift-tab books. In preparing the books, students will develop/improve a variety of skills from following directions to cutting, coloring, and organizing. These books require their participation at many different levels.

Historical facts come alive for a child when reading them from a book he or she helped to create. *U.S. History Little Books: Famous Events* will increase students' history knowledge, fine motor skills, reading abilities, and self esteem.

The *U.S. History Little Books* use the standards on the following page to help foster students' understanding of U. S. History.

Introduction *(cont.)*

Social Studies Standards

The standards listed below are representative of those assigned to kindergarten through 3rd grade students throughout the country.

- ✦ Understands family life now and in the past and family life in various places long ago

The Industrial Revolution—Women's Right to Vote—
Slavery in the United States—The First Thanksgiving

- ✦ Understands the history of a local community and how communities in North America varied long ago

Transportation Firsts—The Civil Rights Movement—
The California Gold Rush —The Invention of the Light Bulb—
The Boston Tea Party

- ✦ Understands the people, events, problems, and ideas that were significant in creating history

The First Inauguration—The Pony Express—The Growth of the U.S.A.

- ✦ Understands how democratic values came to be and how they have been exemplified by people, events, and symbols

The Declaration of Independence—
The Making of the U.S. Constitution—
The Writing of Our National Anthem—The First Thanksgiving

- ✦ Understands the causes and nature of movements of large groups of people into and within the United States, now and long ago

The Oregon Trail—The Growth of the U.S.A.—The California Gold Rush

- ✦ Understands major discoveries in science and technology, some of their social and economic effects, and the major scientists and inventors responsible for them

The Invention of the Light Bulb

How to Use This Book

U.S. History Little Books: Famous Events contains instructions and patterns for primary students to create 16 reproducible books on historical events. There are four different styles of books—folded, layered, pop-up, and lift-tab. Students will find the variety exciting.

This book provides summarized backgrounds of each famous event so that you and your students may have the most basic information as a reference. You should also gather some books from your library and read them to your students. Emphasize the most important points. You may want students to role-play some major events.

Maps are included to give a geographical perspective to students. You may choose to make a transparency of one to share with the group, or you may make hard copies for each student. If you do not have a wall map in the classroom, you may want to enlarge these maps. Encourage students to note the relationship between their homes and the locations of the historical events.

The use of time lines is a way to organize or put events in order. Teachers can introduce the concept by discussing with students the events in their daily life (i.e., get out of bed, eat breakfast, get dressed, go to school, etc.). From there, they can talk in terms of years instead of days (i.e., in what year they, their parents, or their siblings were born).

Some suggestions for using a time line include the following:

- Enlarge the time line from the book and put it on a bulletin board. Highlight each event as it is studied.
- Use floor tape along a wall and write dates along it. Floor tape, like that used on gymnasium floors, will not pull paint off the wall. Place additional pictures of events above the dates.
- Use a clothesline across the classroom and use clothespins to hang events along it.

How to Use This Book *(cont.)*

The parent letter involves the parents in the educational process of their children. It will guide them on how to use the student-made books at home. This is a good way to encourage a strong home-school relationship.

Making books is an excellent culminating project following a unit of study. Children learn valuable reading and social skills and are proud to be able to read their own books to a parent or friend.

Decide whether you want students to create books individually, as part of a group activity, or as a whole-class activity, then make the appropriate number of copies. Once students are familiar with the book-making process, they can learn to write their own innovative versions of newly acquired information.

Individual copies may be used:

- in a reading group.
- as reading homework.
- as a study guide for standardized testing.
- as an extra activity to engage those students who consistently complete their work early.
- as a way to pique interest in students needing motivation.

Group copies may be used:

- as a cooperative learning experience. (Each student prepares a page or two to complete a whole book.)
- to add to the classroom library.
- as a study guide for standardized testing.

Parent Letter

Date:______________________

Dear Parents,

Today your child is bringing home a self-made book. This is just one of many he or she will create during the year. The books will be different in style but all will cover topics of importance in the history of the United States.

These books are for you to enjoy with your child. The books represent social science skills that each student is responsible for mastering. Encourage your child to "read" the book to you. Don't worry if all the words are not right or if the text is memorized. This is how reading begins. Celebrate what your child can do and the interest shown in wanting to read. Along with reading practice, these books can be used to review social studies topics before testing.

Your involvement in your child's academic life is critical to his or her success. The topics covered in the books are interesting and part of our history. You will enjoy reviewing these facts as your child learns about the United States.

Sincerely,

____

Teacher

Time Line

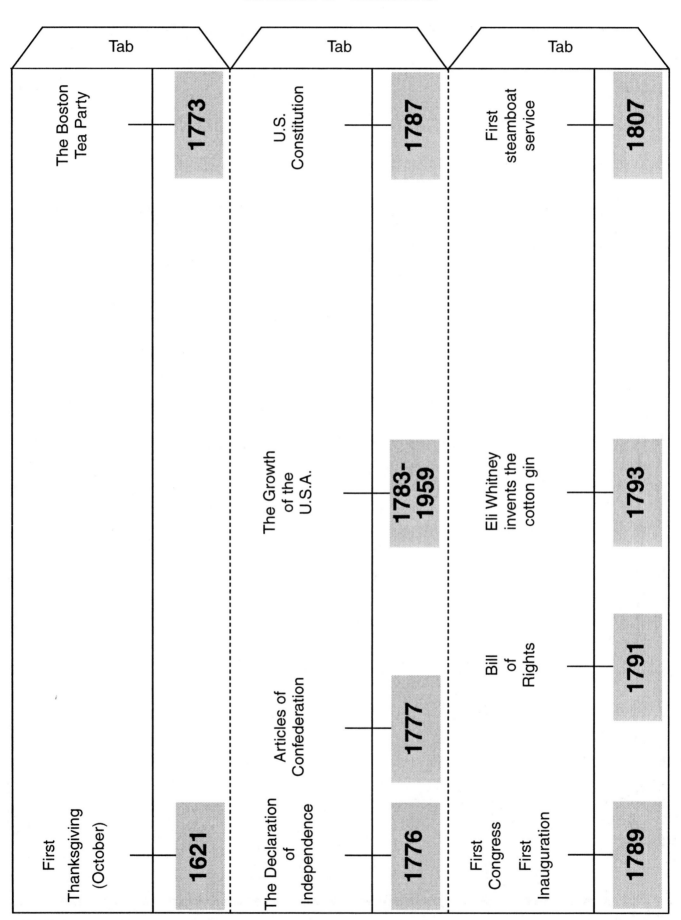

Tab

1621 — First Thanksgiving (October)

1773 — The Boston Tea Party

Tab

1776 — The Declaration of Independence

1777 — Articles of Confederation

1783-1959 — The Growth of the U.S.A.

1787 — U.S. Constitution

Tab

1789 — First Congress; First Inauguration

1791 — Bill of Rights

1793 — Eli Whitney invents the cotton gin

1807 — First steamboat service

 ©Teacher Created Resources, Inc.

Time Line *(cont.)*

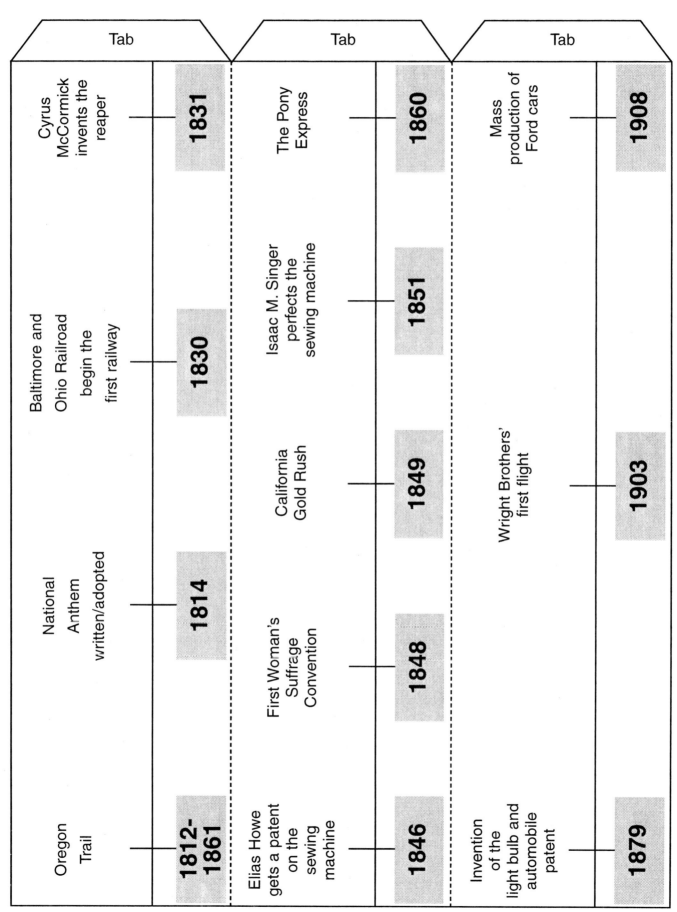

Tab

- **1812-1861** — Oregon Trail
- **1814** — National Anthem written/adopted
- **1830** — Baltimore and Ohio Railroad begin the first railway
- **1831** — Cyrus McCormick invents the reaper

Tab

- **1846** — Elias Howe gets a patent on the sewing machine
- **1848** — First Woman's Suffrage Convention
- **1849** — California Gold Rush
- **1851** — Isaac M. Singer perfects the sewing machine
- **1860** — The Pony Express

Tab

- **1879** — Invention of the light bulb and automobile patent
- **1903** — Wright Brothers' first flight
- **1908** — Mass production of Ford cars

Time Line *(cont.)*

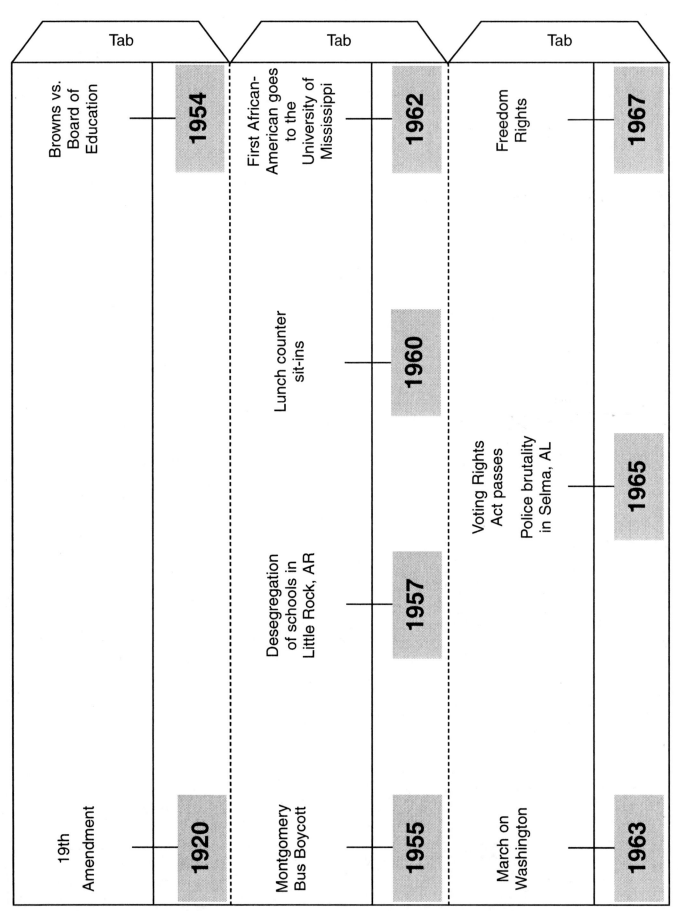

Tab

1920 — 19th Amendment

1954 — Browns vs. Board of Education

Tab

1955 — Montgomery Bus Boycott

1957 — Desegregation of schools in Little Rock, AR

1960 — Lunch counter sit-ins

1962 — First African-American goes to the University of Mississippi

Tab

1963 — March on Washington

1965 — Voting Rights Act passes

Police brutality in Selma, AL

1967 — Freedom Rights

Putting Together Folded Books

Materials

For each student you will need:

- a copy of each of the text pages
- a stapler
- a set of crayons or markers

Assembly Directions for a Folded Book

1. Color each page.*

2. Fold each sheet on the solid line.

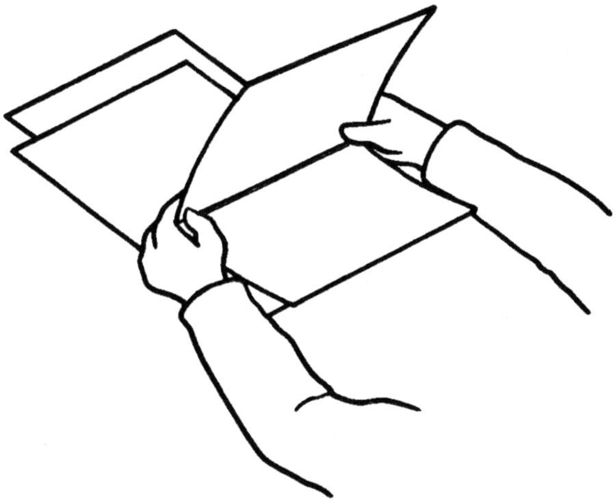

3. Stack the pages in numerical order.

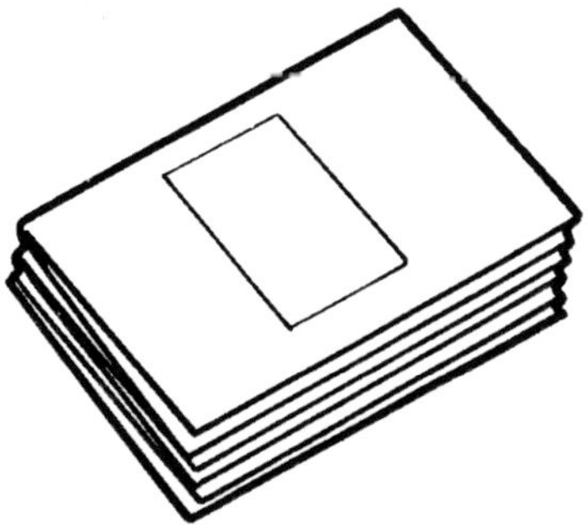

4. Staple down the left side of the booklet.

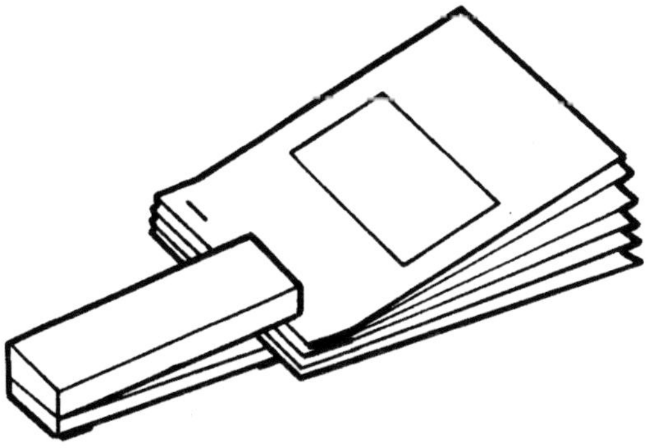

*The picture and text of half of the folded-book page is upside down. This is so that when the page is folded, stacked, and stapled, the book will read correctly.

The First Inauguration

After the Revolutionary War, George Washington just wanted to go home to Mount Vernon in Virginia and spend the rest of his life there with his wife, Martha. The people of the country had other plans for him. A group of electors (not the popular vote) unanimously voted George Washington as the first president in April 1789.

George had a lot of land and a nice house in Fairfax County, Virginia, but he had been away fighting a war. He hadn't had the time to make money on his plantation. He had to borrow 600 pounds from a businessman named Richard Conway who lived in Alexandria, Virginia, in order to make the trip to New York to be sworn in as president.

Mount Vernon was very close to Washington, D.C., but at that time the temporary capital was in New York City. George Washington left home on the long trip on April 16th in order to get to the inauguration that was scheduled for April 30th. Washington did not want celebrations, but it became quite a national event. People met him in every town he went through. Friends and neighbors accompanied him on the first leg of the trip. The people of Georgetown, Virginia, stayed with him until he was met by the people of Baltimore, Maryland. In several cities, he was greeted with parades, banquets, toasts, church bells, and welcoming speeches. In Philadelphia, Washington got out of his carriage, mounted a white horse, and went through archways of flowers lining the route. At Elizabethtown Point, the soon-to-be president got on a barge. Washington's barge was accompanied by other barges filled with members of the Committees of Congress and other important dignitaries. Guns were fired from the shore to salute him as he passed. The governor of New York met Washington at the dock and offered him a carriage but he declined and walked to the house that he was to stay in while in New York. It was called the Franklin House. Washington spent five days at the Franklin House welcoming guests.

On Inauguration Day, Washington wore a dark brown suit and powdered his hair. He did not like to wear wigs. He left the house around noon, accompanied by 500 military men. He rode in a stagecoach to Federal Hall, the meeting place for the new Congress. Federal Hall was built in 1699 and had previously been a courthouse and a jail. The swearing-in took place on a balcony. Washington put his hand on a Masonic Bible, repeated the oath of office read to him by Chancellor Livingston, and at the end Washington added "so help me God" which remains in the oath today. Afterwards, Washington gave his inaugural address that was said to be ten pages long; then he, and others went to St. Paul's Church for religious services.

Some of the traditions established at the first inauguration continue in the inaugurations of today. The swearing-in still takes place outside with the president's hand on a Bible and an inaugural address occurs afterwards followed by a church service and a parade. The American flag is proudly displayed in many locations.

 ©Teacher Created Resources, Inc.

The First Inauguration

Map Study

George Washington traveled from his home at Mount Vernon to New York City for his presidential inauguration.

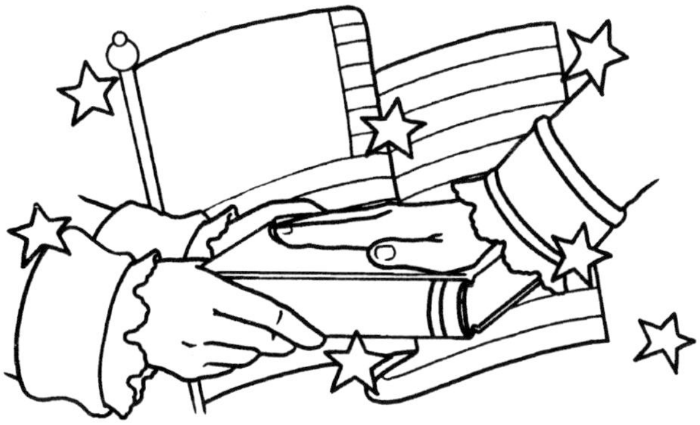

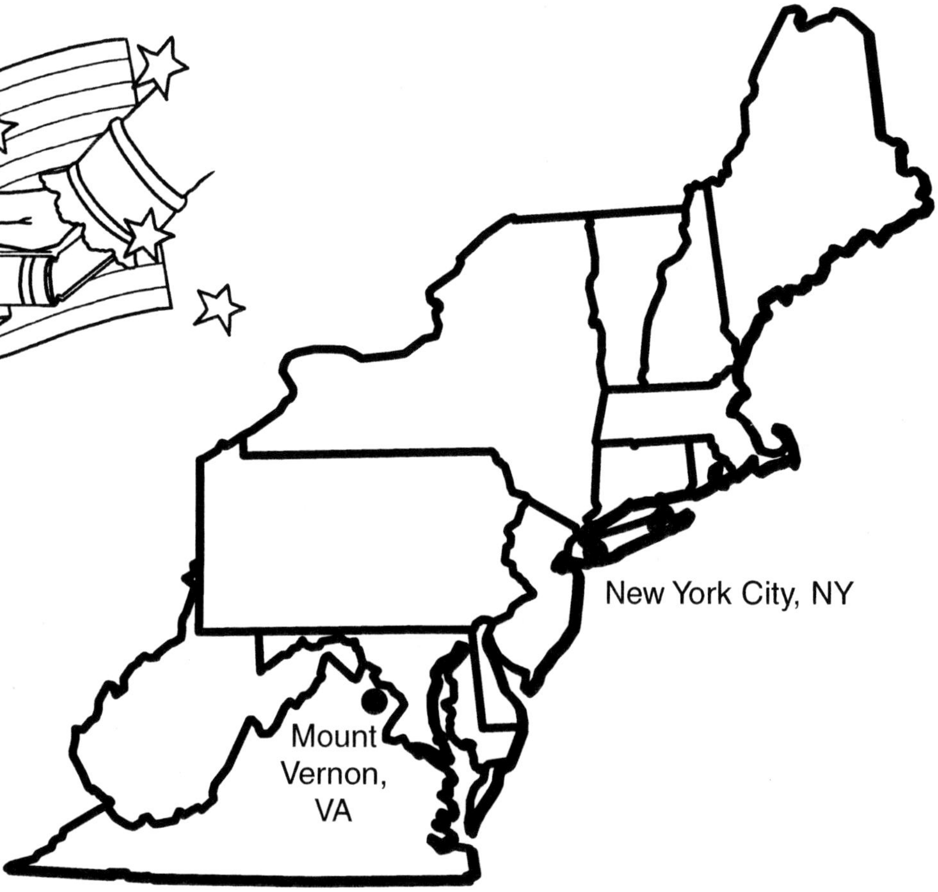

The first inauguration was held in New York City on April 30, 1789. New York City was the temporary capital of the nation. 1

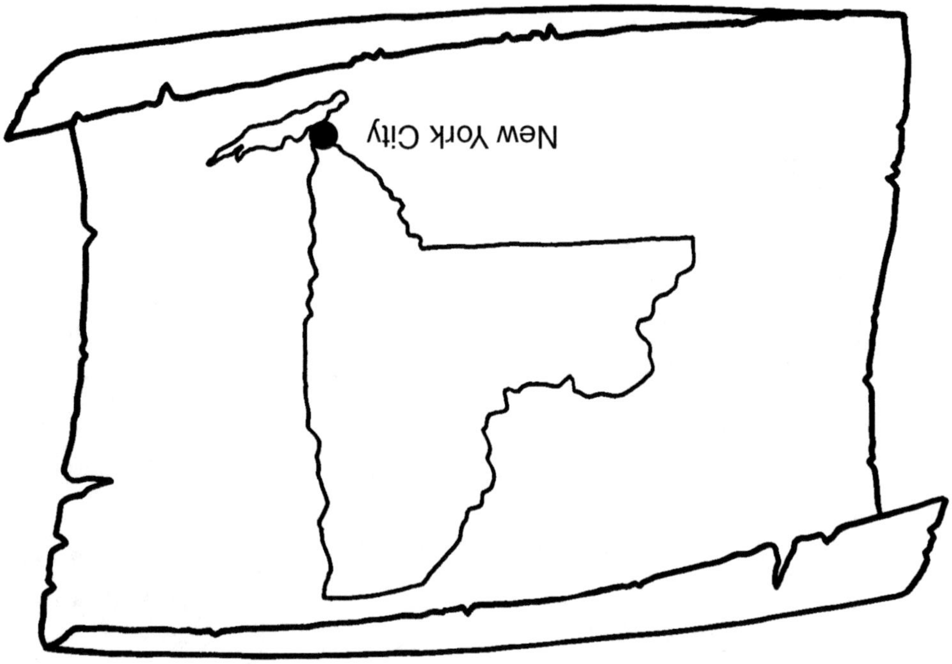

The First Inauguration

 ©Teacher Created Resources, Inc.

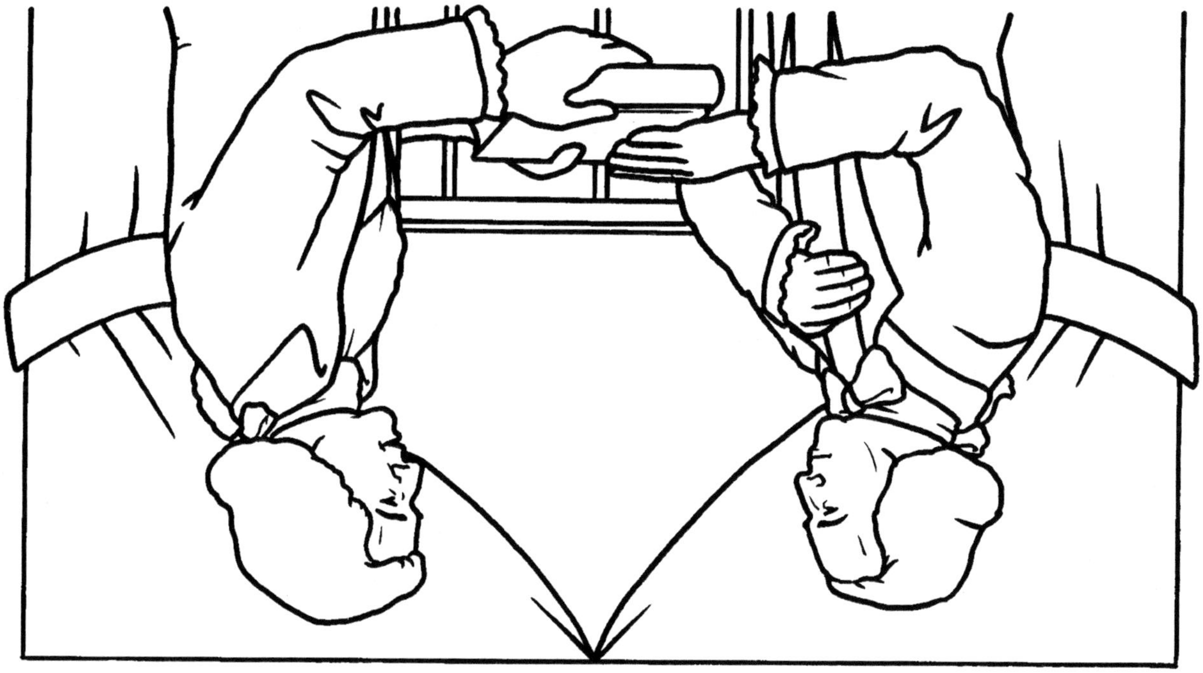

On Inauguration Day, George Washington stood on a balcony, took his oath of office, and then gave the inaugural address. Afterwards, he went to church services and participated in a parade. 3

George Washington reluctantly left his home in Mount Vernon, Virginia. He was greeted by throngs of people along his route to New York City. 2

Many of the traditions established at the first inauguration are still carried on today. 4

The Making of the U.S. Constitution

After the Declaration of Independence was signed, the Articles of Confederation were set up in 1777 to form one nation. This was done to enable the colonies to fight the English. The Articles of Confederation was not a very strong document. After the Revolutionary War, America needed to pay back debts to other countries, to pay the soldiers who had fought in the war, and to help the farmers.

The Articles did not provide a way to raise money. The states started making their own money and arguing with each other about it. Several leaders in the country decided that we had to form a stronger nation with the people in control. The delegates met in May 1787, in what is now Independence Hall in Philadelphia to amend the Articles of Confederation. They worked all summer on a governing plan. It was decided that a new plan was needed. George Washington was selected to be president of the Constitutional Convention.

The first votes were for the Virginia Plan created by Edmund Randolph of Virginia. The Virginia Plan provided for the three branches of government:

- *Legislative branch* to make the laws (Congress)
- *Judicial branch* composed of the court system to make sure people obeyed the laws
- *Executive branch* composed of the president and others to make sure the government ran properly

Next came the compromise. It was decided that Congress would have two houses. To make small states happy, the Senate would be comprised of two representatives from each state. To please the larger states, the House of Representatives would have delegates from each state determined by its population.

The next step was to write a constitution that would have the new laws in it. On September 17, 1787, thirty-nine of the founding fathers, which included George Washington, James Madison, and Benjamin Franklin, signed the completed document. Benjamin Franklin was 81-years-old and the eldest statesman.

A debate began immediately after the U.S. Constitution was signed. The Federalists were for the constitution and a strong national government. The Antifederalists, including Patrick Henry, were more for individual states' rights. Some of the delegates felt that it needed to state the people's rights. When James Madison of Virginia attended the first Congress in 1789, he proposed the Bill of Rights. These ten amendments were added to the Constitution in 1791.

More amendments have since been added to the Constitution. The original document is in the National Archives building in Washington, D.C.

The Making of the U.S. Constitution

Map Study

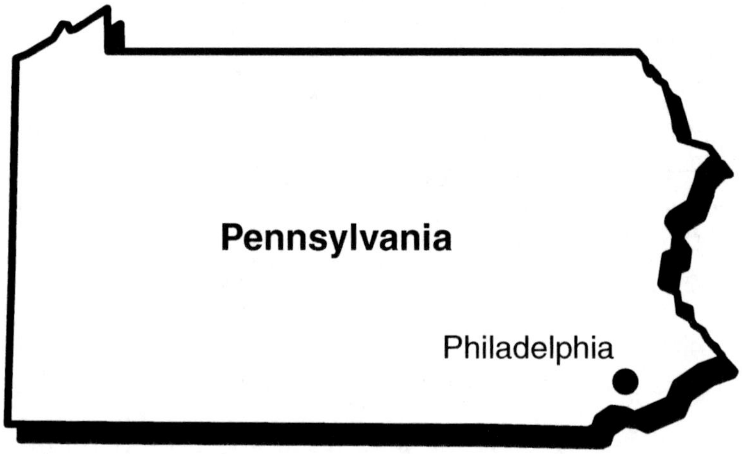

The Constitutional Convention met in Philadelphia, Pennsylvania, in May, 1787.

1

The states began arguing among themselves after the Revolutionary War.

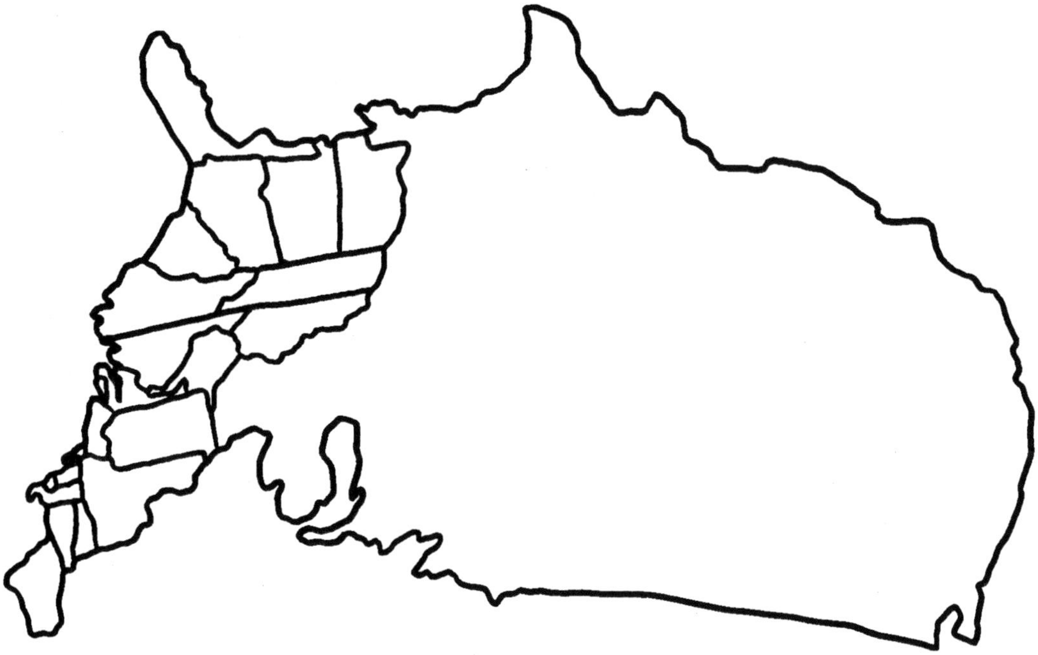

The Making of the U.S. Constitution

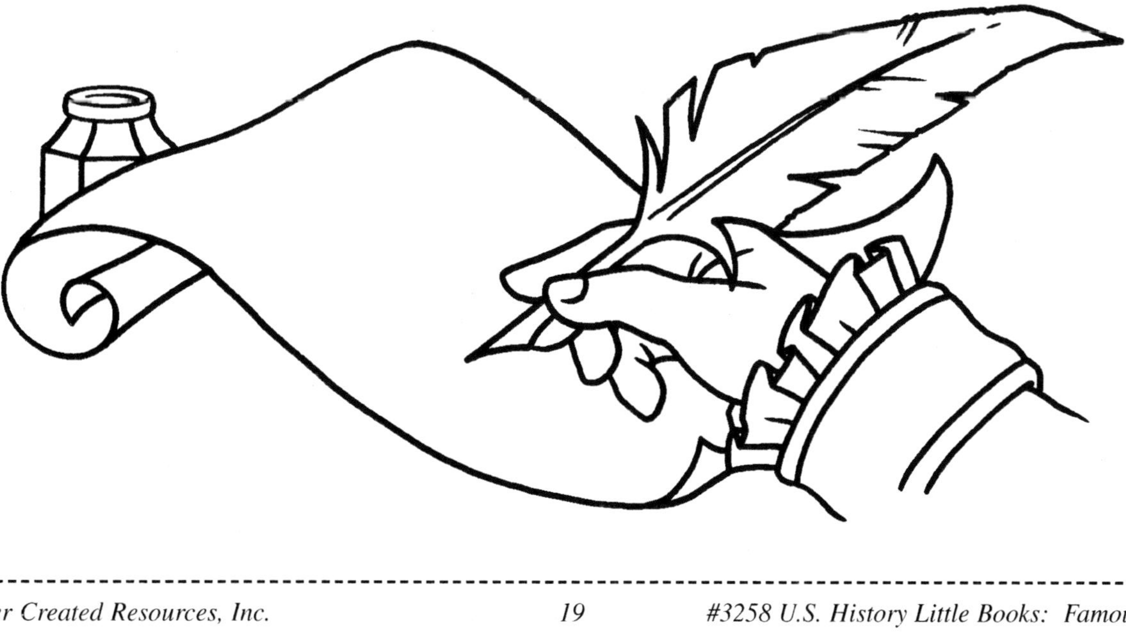

3

The delegates decided to write a new constitution. It was signed on September 17, 1787.

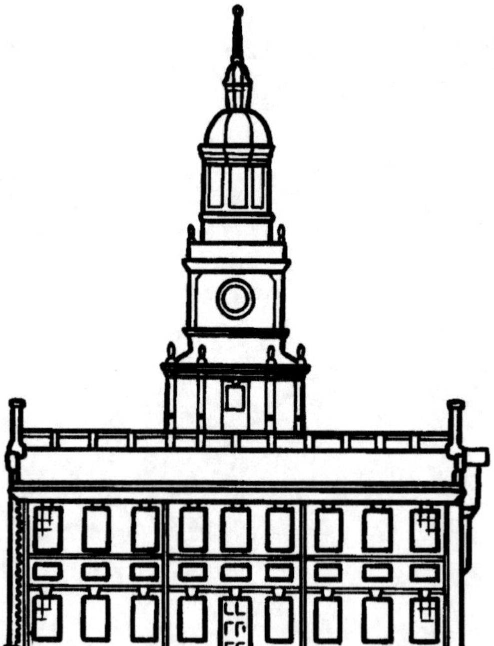

Several leaders decided to meet in Philadelphia to amend the Articles of Confederation in order to have a stronger nation.

2

Twenty-six amendments, including the Bill of Rights, have been added to the Constitution. The original document is displayed in the National Archives building in Washington, D.C.

5

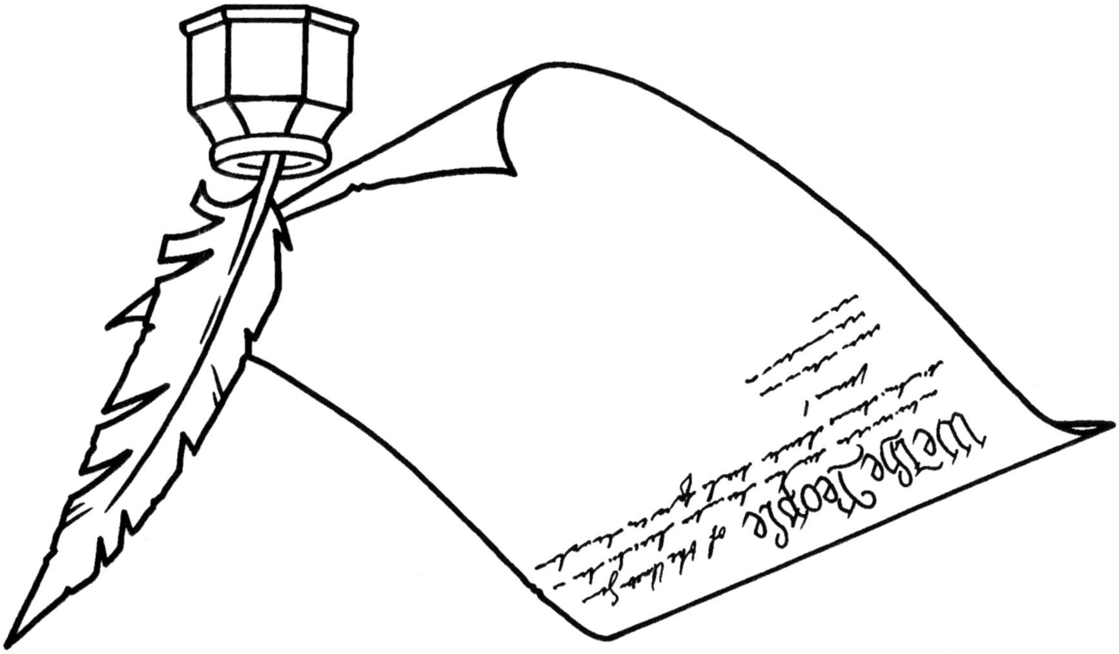

All of the states ratified the Constitution except North Carolina and Rhode Island. However, they both joined later.

4

The Industrial Revolution

The Industrial Revolution was a time of great change in the world. It transformed societies that were predominantely agricultural to ones that were urban. Goods that once were produced one at a time by a few people became ones that were mass-produced by many people working together.

The United States experienced its biggest revolutionary change during the late 1700s through the late 1800s. It was during this time that unclaimed land in the northeast became scarce. Those who wanted farms were moving west. Many opportunities for those remaining were in industry.

Eli Whitney invented the cotton gin, increasing 50 times the speed at which cotton fiber was milled. Elias Howe and Isaac Singer shared in the invention and perfection of the sewing machine. Cyrus McCormick invented reapers for those who wanted to harvest produce with greater efficiency. Henry Ford invented the Model T so that others besides the wealthy could own automobiles. All of these inventions made possible the mass-production of fabrics, crops, and cars. And with those inventions came new job opportunities in mills for hundreds of people.

Quite often, a mill owner built housing for his employees. He provided a company store in which employees could purchase supplies they needed using credits they earned at work. Though this was a convenient way for employees to live, their choices were limited and many people eventually found themselves obligated to the mill and indebted to the mill owner. Once the employees were locked into the mill jobs and homes, the mill owners did not always make the proper repairs to their residences. Many workers toiled 12 hours a day, six days a week. Working and living conditions were poor, and there was little hope of improvement.

Before the Industrial Revolution, children had worked hard on family farms. They, too, transitioned from agricultural to industrial work. Many worked as many hours as the adults, doing hard, dangerous labor in the factories. It was not until early in the 20th century that labor laws were put in place to protect children's rights. Even with these laws, children worked in factories as late as the year 1938.

Eventually, workers formed unions to protect the rights of the employees. Conditions began to improve at the workplace, as did production. The Industrial Revolution brought changes, problems, and opportunities for citizens of the United States that our forefathers could never have imagined. Today, the United States produces goods that are exported all over the world.

 ©Teacher Created Resources, Inc.

The Industrial Revolution

Map Study

The Industrial Revolution began in the northern United States.

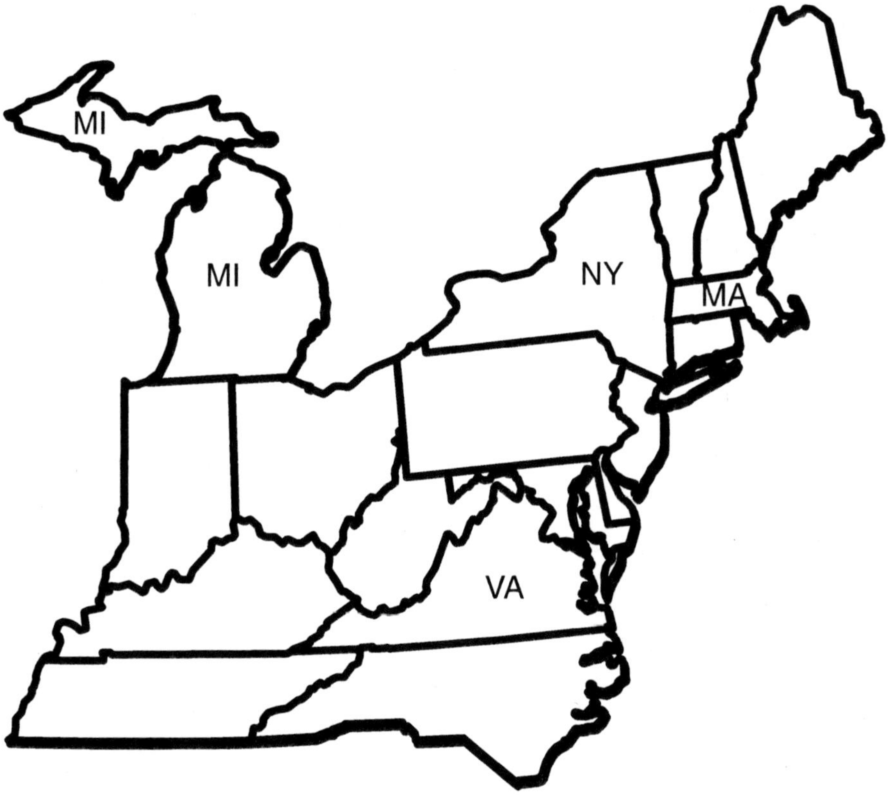

The Industrial Revolution changed the United States from a land of agriculture to a land of industry. People learned how to mass-produce goods in factories.

1

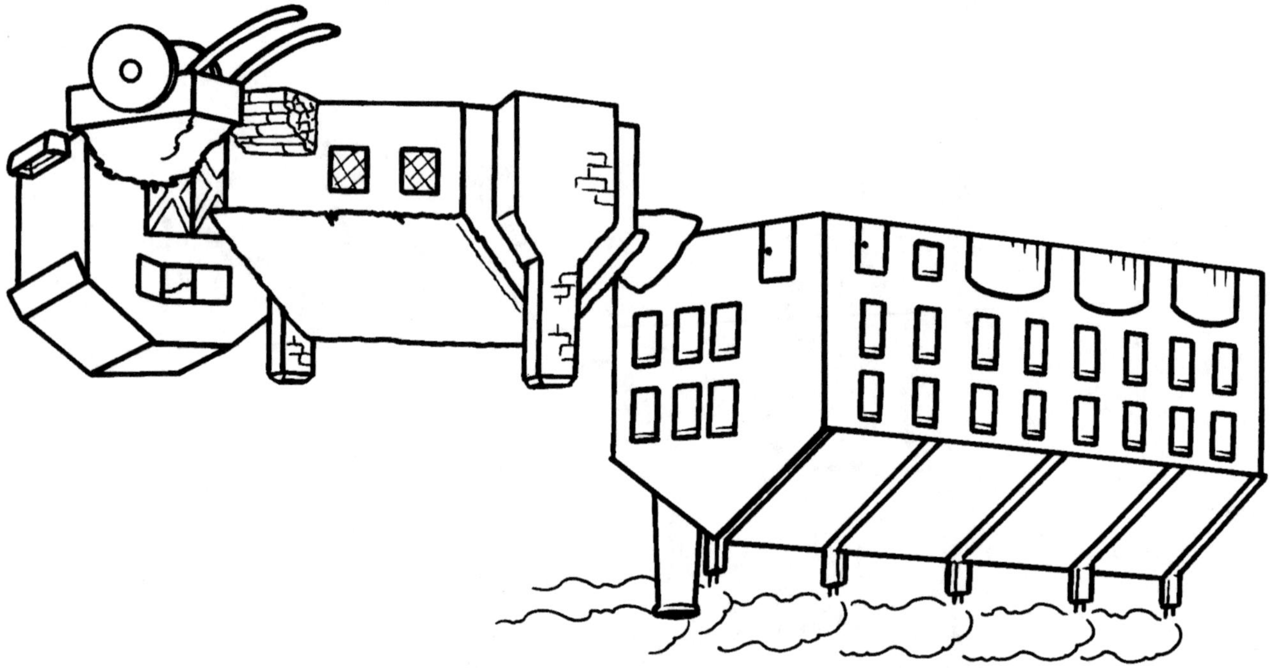

The Industrial

Revolution

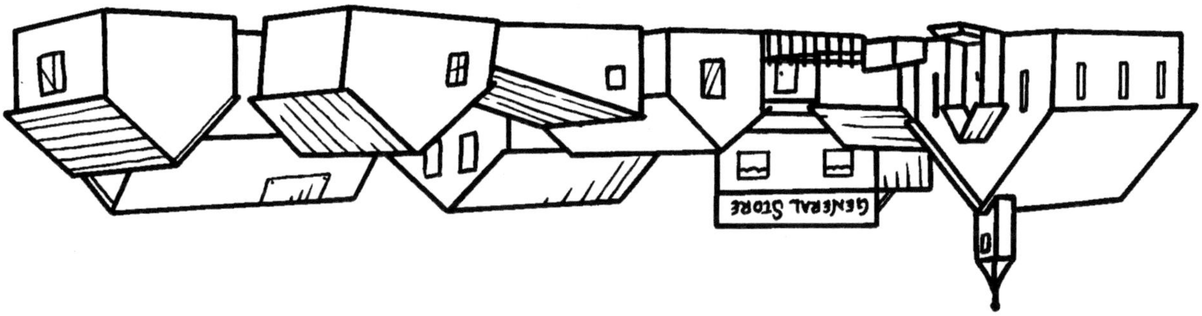

Mill owners provided housing and a company store for their employees. However, the living and working conditions were not very nice.

3

Many inventors came up with faster ways of producing goods. Eli Whitney made the cotton gin, Elias Howe and Isaac Singer introduced the sewing machine, and Cyrus McCormick designed a crop harvester.

2

Child labor laws were put into place so children were no longer forced to work in the factories. Conditions improved. The United States has remained a productive, industrialized nation.

5

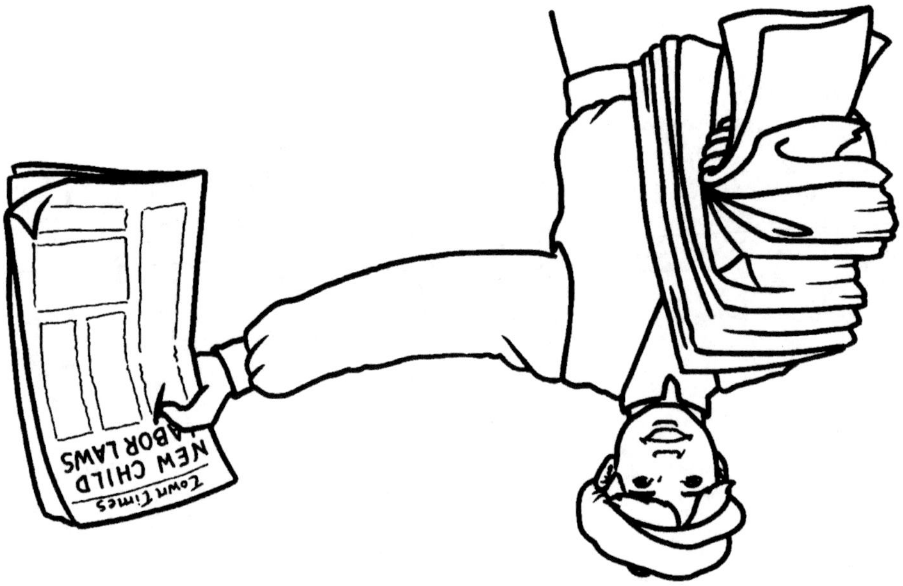

Children worked hard too. They didn't get to play or go to school. Eventually, labor unions formed to protect the rights of workers.

4

Women's Right to Vote

Historically, women have not had the same rights as men. European and American law was based upon ancient Roman laws, which said that husbands owned their wives. Because women were considered property, they were not allowed to vote. When the American colonies were forming, some women were allowed to vote because they owned property. Later on, it was left up to the states to decide who could vote. It was decided that only men would have this privilege.

Suffrage is the right of women to vote and to hold political office. The suffrage movement for women began in the late 1800s. This evolved from the *abolitionist movement* (banning slavery) and the *temperance movement* (banning alcohol). Susan B. Anthony, a suffragette, began an organization called the Women's State Temperance Society of New York. Because many people in the temperance and abolitionist societies were anti-feminists, Susan B. Anthony joined with Elizabeth Cady Stanton and Lucretia Mott to form another organization, the National Woman Suffrage Association. Elizabeth Cady Stanton was such a strong believer in feminist views that she refused to have the word "obey" in her wedding vows when she married her husband. She became the first president of the National Woman Suffrage Association (NWSA).

In 1848, the National Woman Suffrage Association held the Seneca Falls Convention. The Declaration of Sentiments was adopted declaring women as equals of men. It was written with some of the same language that was used in the Declaration of Independence. Many people were angry about this convention, which resulted in some violence.

After the Civil War, the abolitionists wanted ex-slaves to have the right to vote. However, they didn't deem the women's suffrage issues as important. During this period, Lucy Stone emerged as a strong feminist. When she married, she kept her maiden name. When other women did the same, they were called "Lucy Stoners." In 1869, Lucy Stone and Julia Ward Howe formed another group called the American Woman Suffrage Association (AWSA).

The movement to secure voting rights for women was further advanced in 1873, when two important cases were presented in court. First, Carrie Burnham, a teacher and a doctor, argued for her right to vote in the Pennsylvania Supreme Court. Later, Susan B. Anthony argued that the language in the 14th Amendment that had statements about the equal rights of citizens gave women the right to vote. Susan B. Anthony lost her court case, but, fourteen years after she died, the Congress of the United States passed the 19th Amendment giving women the right to vote. The year was 1920.

Today, democratic countries in the world allow almost all citizens to vote. The mentally ill and felons are usually not allowed voting rights. Some countries still have certain qualifications that must be met. Property ownership, religion, race, education, age, and even gender can determine who gets the voting privilege.

Women's Right to Vote

Map Study

Many leaders of the women's suffrage movement were situated in the northeastern states.

 ©Teacher Created Resources, Inc.

For many years, women did not have as many rights as male citizens of the United States.

5

Women's Right to Vote

Initially, women's suffrage groups formed from temperance and abolitionist groups.

3

Suffrage is the right of women to vote and hold political office.

2

The Seneca Falls Convention held in 1848 was the first large gathering of the National Woman Suffrage Association.

5

Leaders of the women's suffrage movement were Lucy Stone, Susan B. Anthony, Elizabeth Cady Stanton, and Lucretia Mott.

4

These women picketed, gave great speeches, and wrote in feminists' journals about their cause. 7

We demand
fair treatment.
Organize!

Carrie Burnham and Susan B. Anthony argued in court that women should have the right to vote. 6

Finally, in 1920, Congress passed the 19th Amendment that gave women the right to vote. 8

Putting Together Pop-up Books

Materials for all Pop-up Books:

For each student you will need:

- copies of text and illustrations
- markers or crayons
- scissors
- glue
- 9" x 12" construction paper for cover

Assembly Directions

1. Color the illustrations.

2. Cut out the illustrations on the dashed lines.

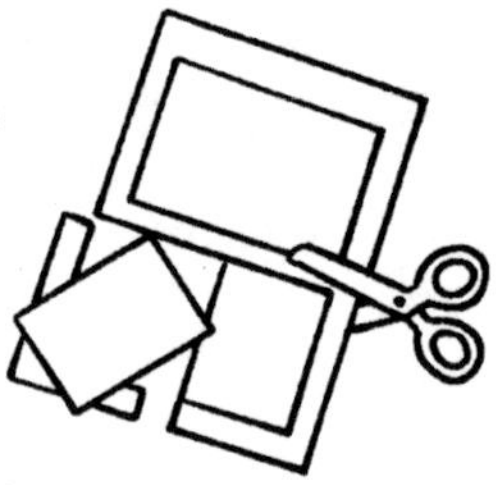

3. Fold a piece of construction paper in half to serve as the front and back covers of the book.

4. Cut out and glue the cover page to the center-front of the book cover.

5. Fold each interior page in half on the solid line. The top of the page should be folded to the back so that the dashed lines are visible for cutting.

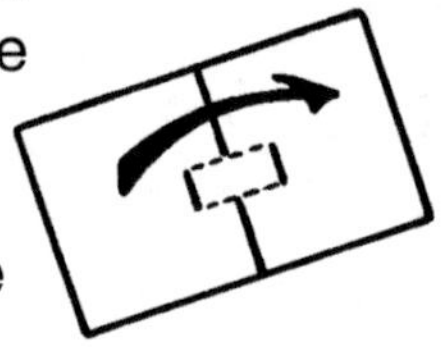

6. Cut along the dashed lines, being sure to cut through both layers of the folded paper. Cut all the way to the large dots.

7. Open the page and fold it back the other way, holding the cut section between your fingers, keeping it folded. Close the page, flattening the cut part so that when you re-open the page, it will be "popped up."

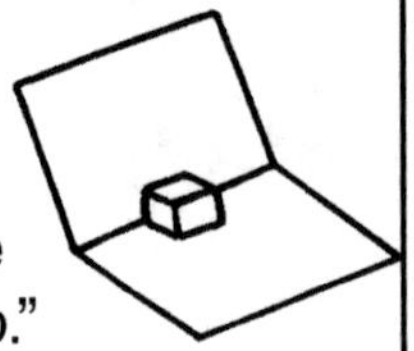

8. Spread glue over the gray box and attach the illustration. **Note:** In order to ensure that the illustration does not bend when the book closes, glue it so it extends above the pop-up.

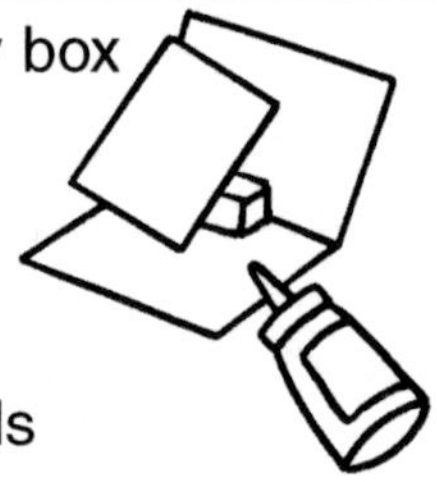

9. Arrange the pages in numerical order. Glue the back of one page to the front of the other until all are together as a booklet.

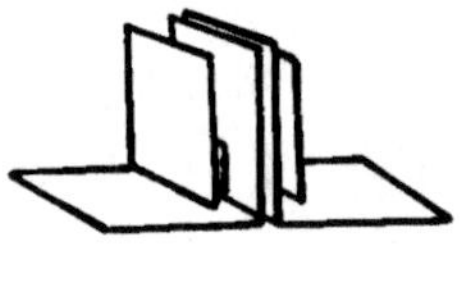

10. Glue the booklet to the inside of the cover.

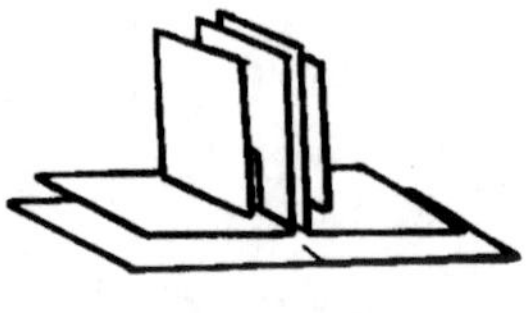

Slavery in the United States

Slavery in the United States of America began shortly after the first settlers came to Jamestown, Virginia. In 1619 some Dutch merchants brought 20 African slaves over and sold them to the colonists to help them on their farms. Eventually, there were slaves all over the 13 colonies. However, the increase in industry in the north led to the need for fewer slaves to do the work. As the British demand for tobacco increased, more acres of southern land were used for its growth, and more and more slaves were bought and sold in the South. For over 200 years, slavery was vital to the economic system in the confederate states.

Slave owners had a belief that the slaves were unable to care for themselves and, therefore, needed to be under the supervision of white men. The slaves were bought and sold like cattle; the buyers checked their teeth and looked them over carefully in an attempt to find the strongest workers. Slaves were viewed as the property of the plantation owner who thought nothing of making them live in dirt-floor shacks with few clothes and a scarce amount of food. It was commonplace for plantation overseers to separate slave families and sell them to various other owners.

Freedom was the only dream for many, many African slaves. By the early 1800s, it was not only the slaves who believed they should be freed. There were various others (abolitionists) who believed that slavery was wrong. They wanted to at least keep it from expanding westward, and hopefully end it altogether. In 1830, slave Nat Turner led an uprising against the white plantation owners and their families. Many people were killed. This action, along with the publication of the books, *American Slavery As It Is*, and *Uncle Tom's Cabin*, heightened citizens' awareness about slavery. As a result, those in support grew more defensive about slavery and those opposed became more vocal.

The creation of the Republican Party in the mid-1850s came as a direct result of the opposition of slavery. The Republicans wanted Abraham Lincoln as their representative. Those in favor of slavery chose Stephen A. Douglas. The two ran for the Senate in 1858. Though Lincoln lost to Douglas in the Senate race, he won against him in the presidential election of 1860. In 1861, eleven states had pulled away from the union to form their own confederacy. Lincoln did not want a divided nation, nor did he want to force people to abolish slavery. He wanted the people to decide against slavery themselves.

Civil War broke out between the North and the South in 1861 and went on until 1865. The North prevailed, the Southern states rejoined the Union, and the 13th Amendment to the Constitution was added, making it against the law to practice slavery. Though it would take a hundred more years for African Americans to be given their full rights as equal U.S. citizens, the end of slavery was a giant step toward their equality.

Although laws today are in place to make the United States a place of equality for all people, it is still a country where prejudices and distrust remain in existence between the races. The United States is still suffering the effects of slavery practiced so long ago.

Slavery in the United States

Map Study

The "striped" states were slave states before the Civil War.

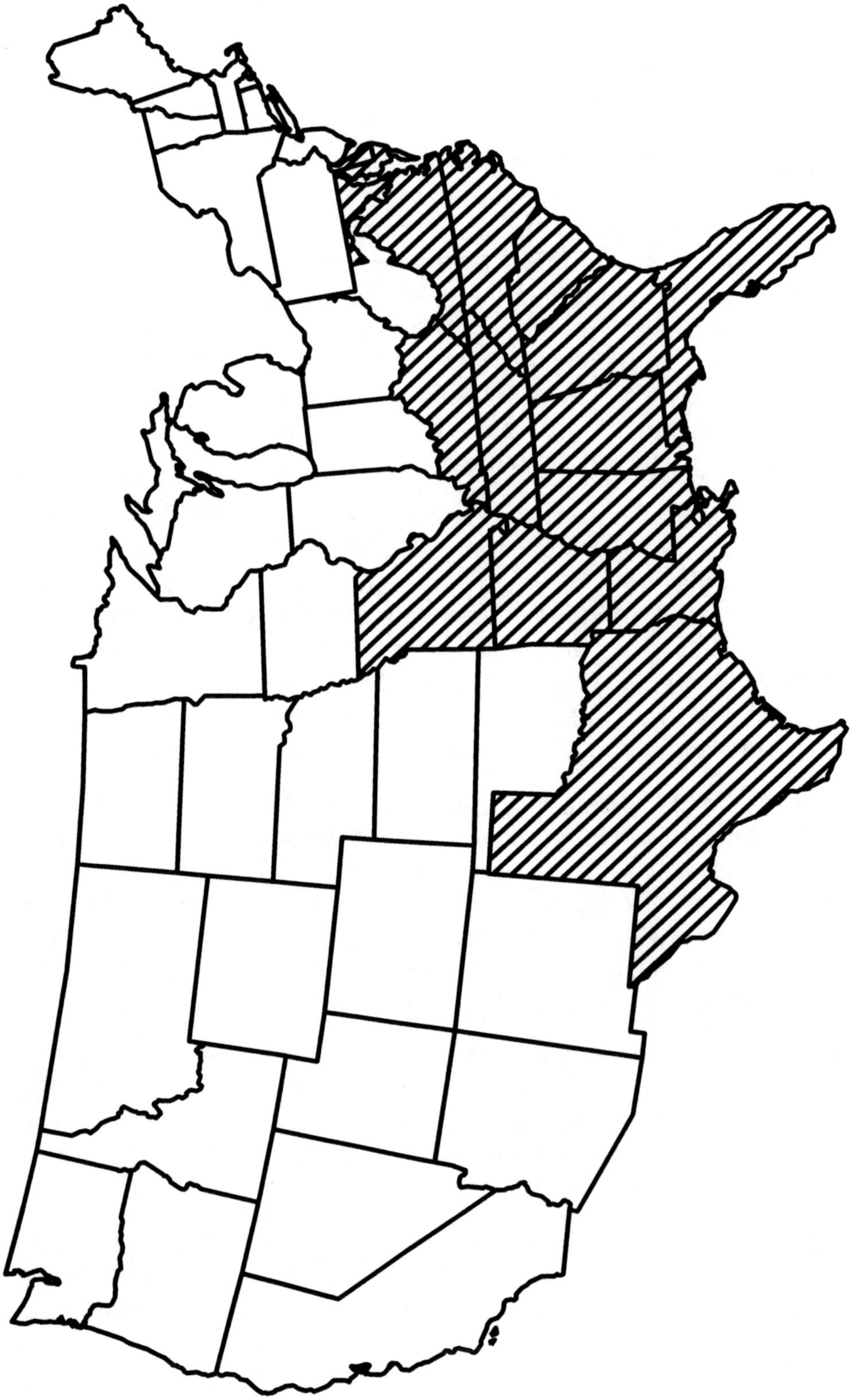

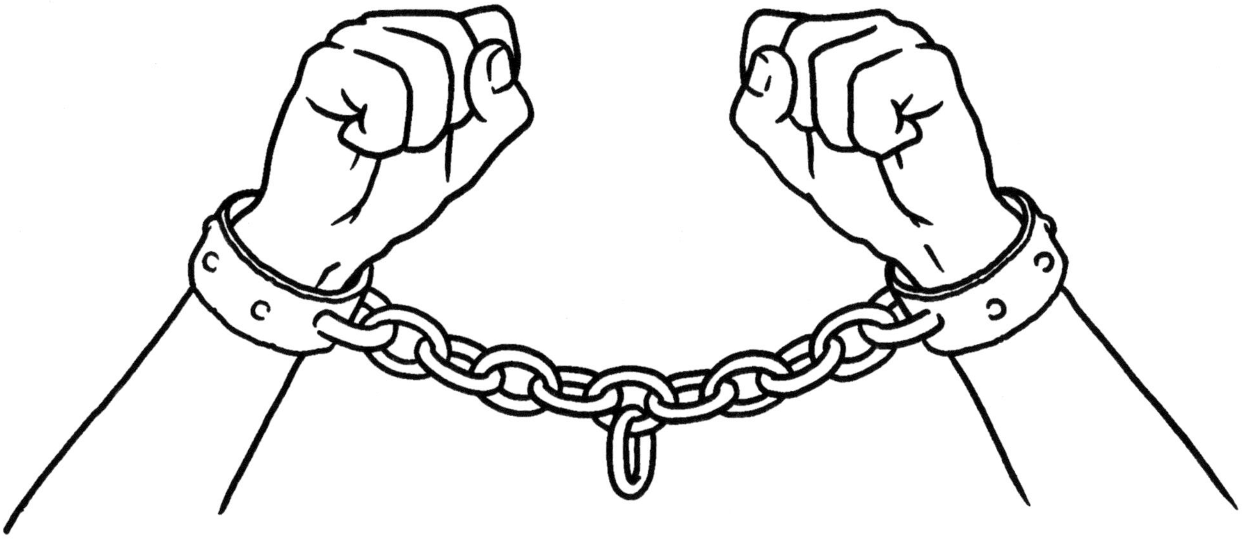

Slavery in the United States

Cover page

Illustrations for pages 1 and 2.

page 1

page 2

Glue

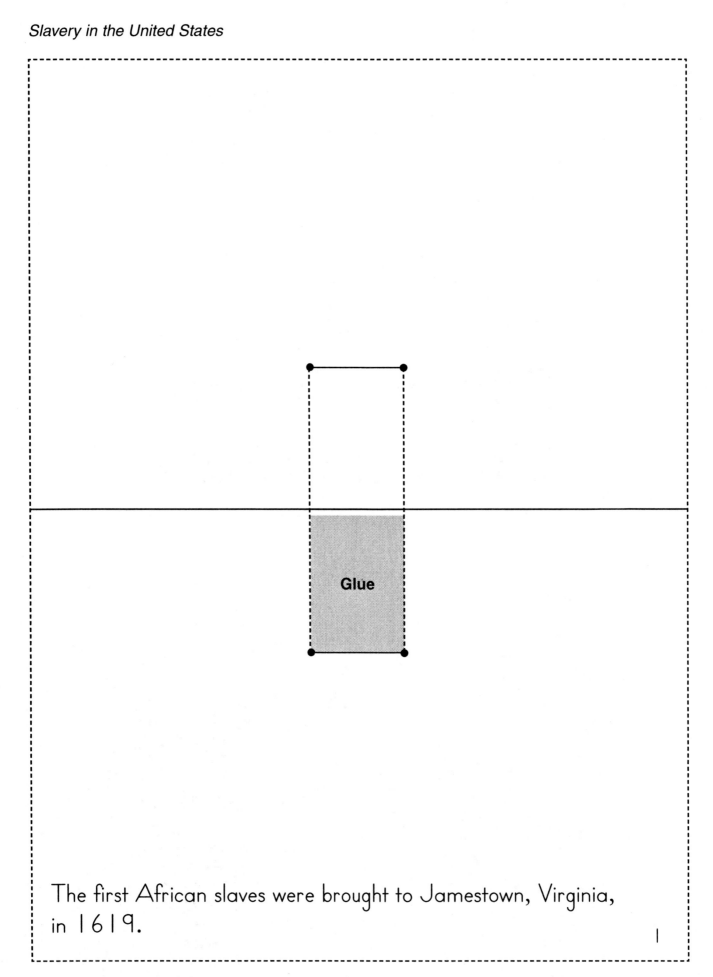

The first African slaves were brought to Jamestown, Virginia, in 1619.

1

 ©Teacher Created Resources, Inc.

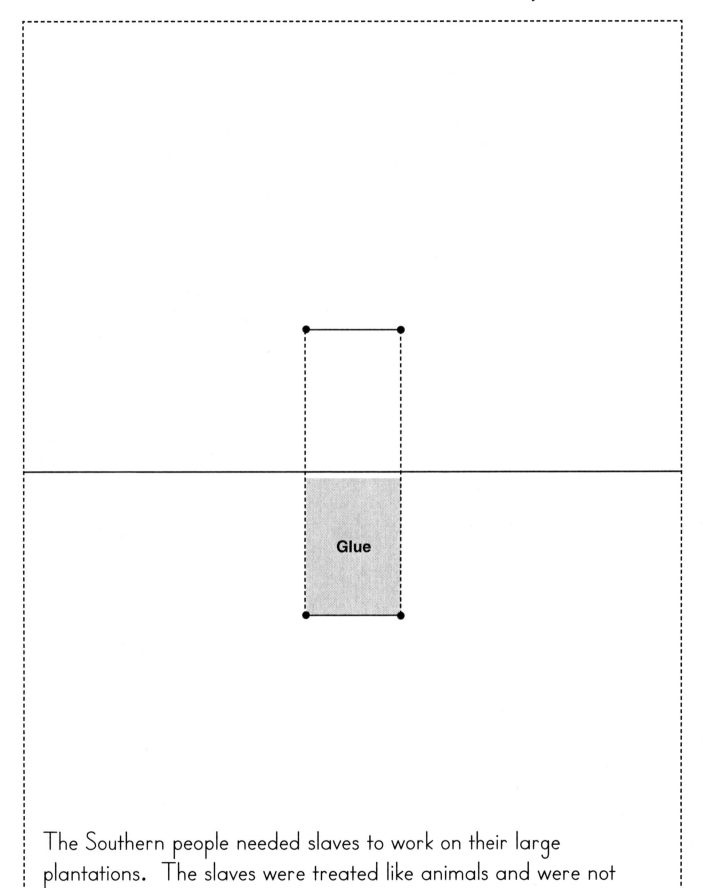

Glue

The Southern people needed slaves to work on their large plantations. The slaves were treated like animals and were not allowed to have basic human rights.

2

Glue

Some white people did not like slavery and believed that the slaves should be freed. In 1861, when Abraham Lincoln was president, a war broke out between the people of the North, who believed slavery was wrong, and the people of the South, who depended on slaves to tend their fields. 3

 ©Teacher Created Resources, Inc.

Glue

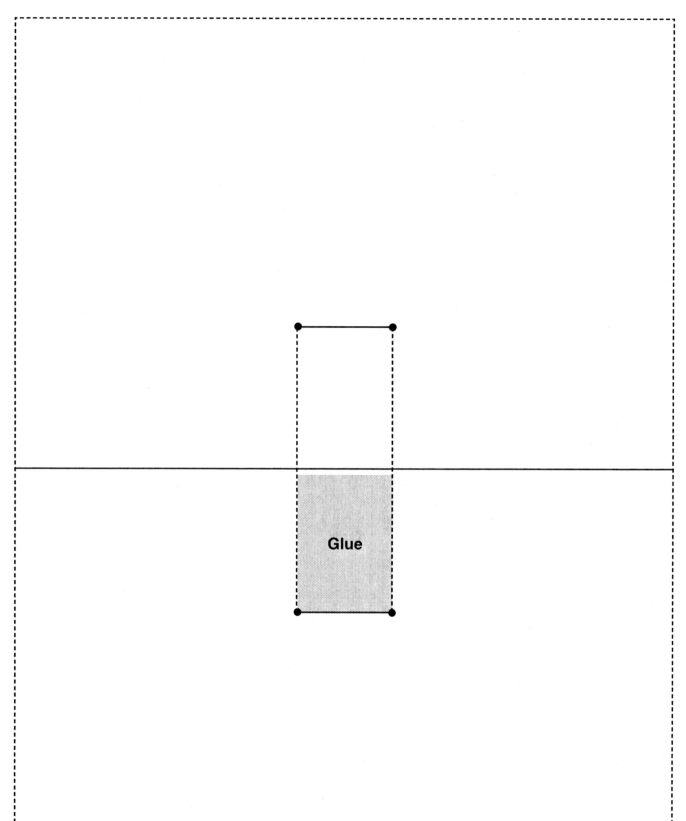

The North won the Civil War. The 13th Amendment was added to the United States Constitution making slavery illegal. Slaves were freed in 1865.

4

Slavery in the United States

Illustrations for pages 3 and 4

page 3

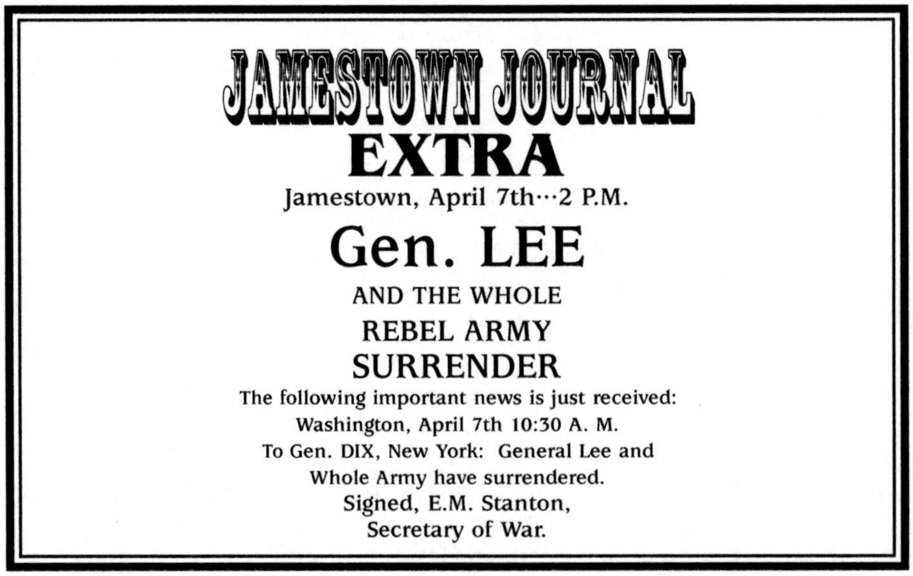

JAMESTOWN JOURNAL
EXTRA
Jamestown, April 7th···2 P.M.
Gen. LEE
AND THE WHOLE
REBEL ARMY
SURRENDER
The following important news is just received:
Washington, April 7th 10:30 A. M.
To Gen. DIX, New York: General Lee and
Whole Army have surrendered.
Signed, E.M. Stanton,
Secretary of War.

page 4

 ©Teacher Created Resources, Inc.

The Declaration of Independence

Thomas Jefferson was a scientist, an attorney, and an architect. He was also a statesman who spent many long hours thinking about what was fair and just for all people. One day in 1770, Sam Howell, who was a slave, came in to ask for Mr. Jefferson's help. He said that there was a law stating that if a master owned slaves, he then owned the children of those slaves. This man's grandmother had been a slave, as had his mother. He told Mr. Jefferson that his grandmother had told him all along that this law didn't extend to him, a grandson, and that he should be a free man. Sam was about to sue his master for his own freedom.

This idea intrigued Thomas Jefferson. For he believed that there was a larger law, one under God, whereby all men were created equal. Thomas Jefferson agreed to take this man's case. The judge in the case was nothing less than astonished that Thomas Jefferson would plead such a case. He threw the case out. However, some people were moved by his earnest argument and they knew that Thomas Jefferson was a man of the highest principles.

Later, in the spring of 1774, Thomas Jefferson was still concerned about the rights of people. He wrote a pamphlet entitled *A Summary View of the Rights of British America* that stated that all men should have the right to make their own laws because the law of nature gives them that right; i.e., when God gives a man life, he also gives him liberty. This pamphlet was circulated through the colonies and Britain. Mr. Jefferson's writings were controversial and made many people curious about him.

There were problems about taxation between Britain and the colonies. The people of Massachusetts were about to suffer great consequences as a result of the Boston Tea Party. King George was angry and had threatened to cut off the port on which they depended for their trade.

The Revolutionary War began between the British and the American Continentals in April of 1775. It went on for a year or so without much progress. The Continental Congress felt that it was of dire importance to let the King of Britain know that the colonists intended to make themselves a free nation. It was decided at a meeting to secure a representative from each colony and have them form a committee to write up some sort of declaration to submit to the king. The colonists needed to send a message that they were one unit.

The Declaration of Independence *(cont.)*

Jefferson was chosen to represent Virginia. He was one of the youngest in the group, but was proud to be among such greats as John Adams and Benjamin Franklin. He fully assumed that the task of writing would go to an older gentleman with more experience, John Adams. He was pleasantly surprised when John Adams declined, stating that since Virginia was the most populous colony, the author should be a Virginian. Adams acknowledged that he, himself, was not a popular man, and that Thomas Jefferson could write 10 times better than he could.

Mr. Jefferson took his new role very seriously. After a lot of thought, he sat down and put together a large portion of the Declaration of Independence in one sitting. He spent the next several days making improvements. His document was then edited by the other committee members who removed the parts that referred to slavery. They came to an agreement, and on July 4, 1776, the Declaration of Independence was adopted by the Continental Congress. It was signed first by John Hancock, then by the other 55 members. The Declaration of Independence contains principles by which our country has lived for more than 200 years.

Each year on the Fourth of July, the United States of America celebrates the adoption of The Declaration of Independence. There are parades through the town squares, picnics for families and friends, and great fireworks displays after dark. Our country uses this day to remember Thomas Jefferson and those people of 1776 who believed that ours was a nation of freedom.

 ©Teacher Created Resources, Inc.

The Declaration of Independence

Map Study

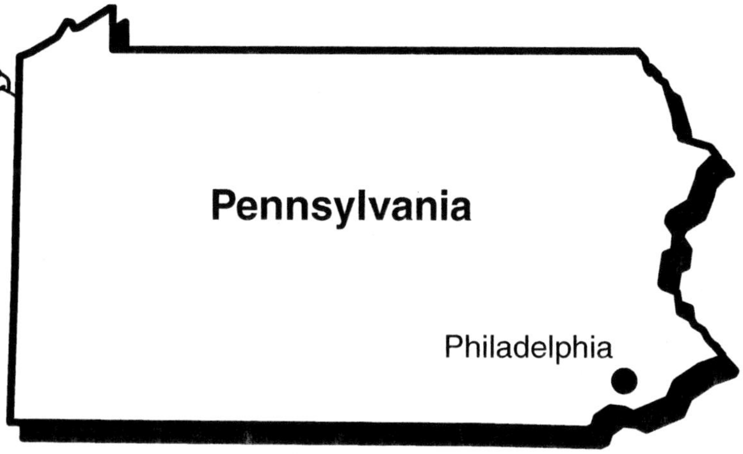

The Declaration of Independence was adopted on July 4, 1776. It was signed in Philadelphia.

Cover page

Illustrations for pages 1 and 2.

page 1

page 3

 ©Teacher Created Resources, Inc.

Glue

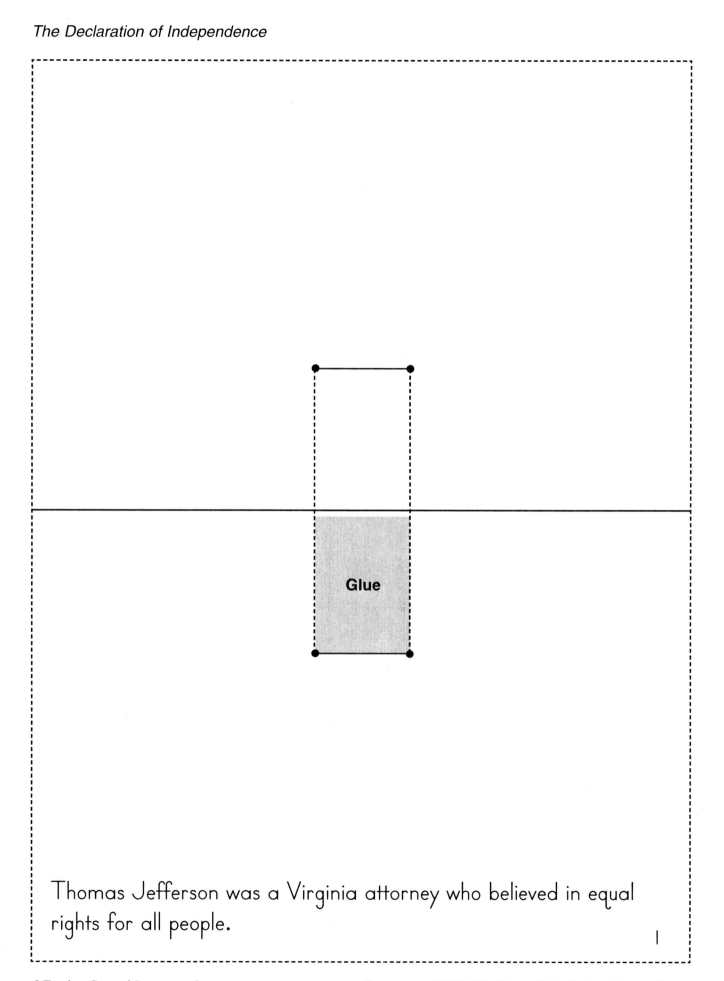

Thomas Jefferson was a Virginia attorney who believed in equal rights for all people.

1

Glue

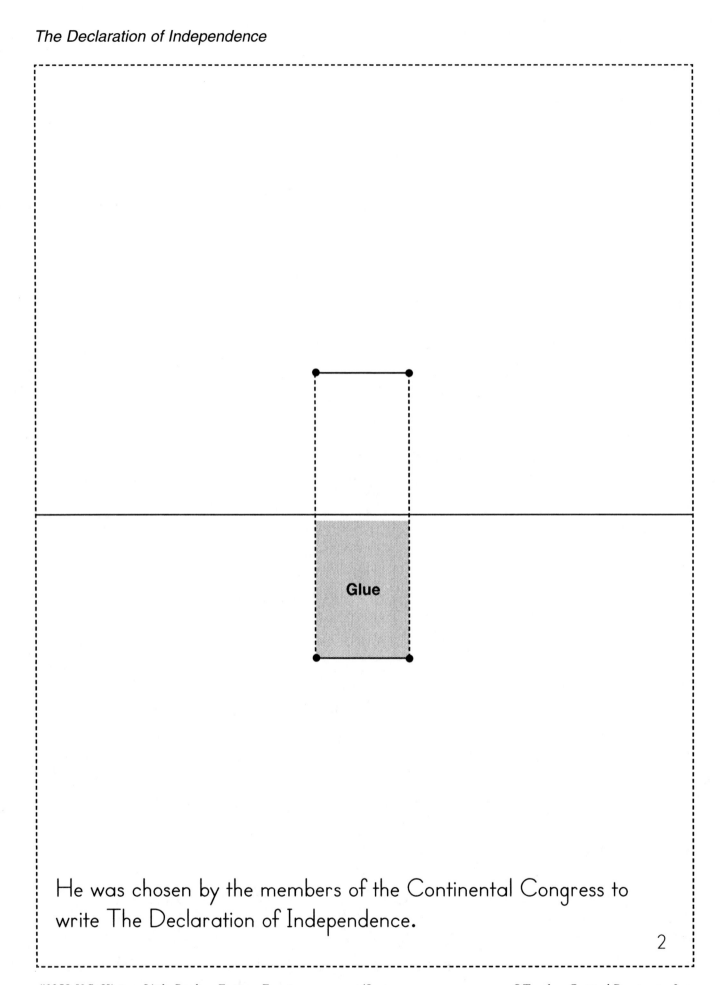

He was chosen by the members of the Continental Congress to write The Declaration of Independence.

2

 ©Teacher Created Resources, Inc.

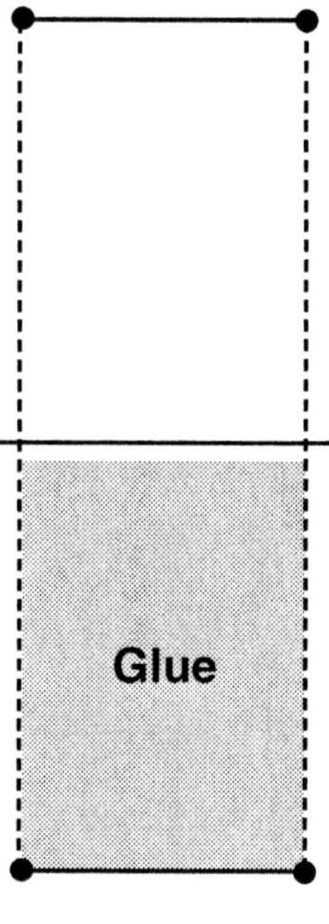

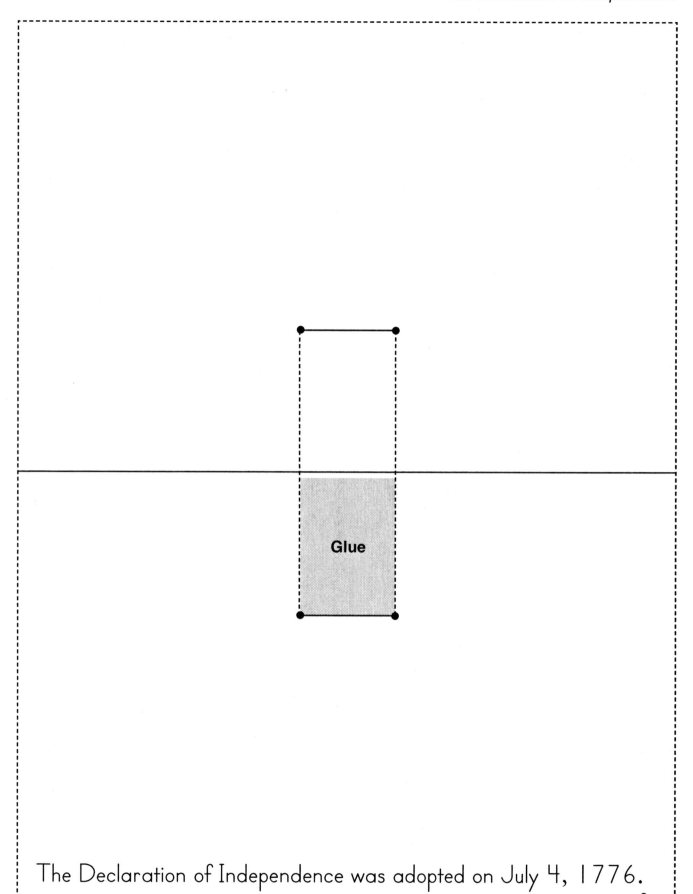

The Declaration of Independence was adopted on July 4, 1776.

3

Americans celebrate the adoption of The Declaration of Independence on the Fourth of July each year. There are picnics with family and friends, parades through town squares, and fireworks displays after dark.

4

 ©Teacher Created Resources, Inc.

The Declaration of Independence

Illustrations for pages 2 and 4

page 2

page 4

The Invention of the Light Bulb

Many people had seen the need for electric lights for years. An electrical engineer from Russia had invented large arc lights by having an arc of electricity jump between two wires. The problem was that they produced a light that was blinding. Thomas Alva Edison wanted to find a way to make lights that one could use in a small area, such as a house. He wanted to create an affordable light source for the average person's home.

Thomas Edison had made enough money from his inventions that he built a large laboratory in Menlo Park, New Jersey. This laboratory became the first to be used for industrial research in the world. He knew that if electricity could light up the sky during a storm, that he ought to be able to use it to light up houses. First he made a glass bulb. Then Mr. Edison started trying different types of wires that would glow for a long time and resist the high temperatures in the bulb. He sent several of his employees to the Amazon and to Japan looking for ingredients for the wire or filament. He experimented with fishing line and coconut hair. He even tried the red hair from the beard of a man!

One night Mr. Edison rolled lampblack or soot and tar to form a wire and put it in the bulb. It glowed when electricity was turned on. These ingredients glowed for just a short while. He thought it burned out quickly because it had air in it, so he looked for something that had no air.

On October 19, 1879, Thomas Edison used carbonized thread (burned cotton sewing thread) as a filament in the bulb. It glowed! Mr. Edison would not go to sleep or leave the bulb because he wanted to know exactly how long it would last. The bulb went out after 40 hours. It was the first incandescent light, or light produced from heat, that lasted a long time with a small amount of electricity. He kept experimenting with different filaments and finally settled on carbonized bamboo.

Shortly afterwards, Mr. Edison started a light bulb factory and designed an electric power station so electricity would be available to all people. The Edison Electric Lighting Company started operating the first power station in the world in London in 1882. Later that year the first permanent generating station in the United States was established in New York City.

After the invention of the light bulb, Edison was known around the world as "The Wizard of Menlo Park."

 ©Teacher Created Resources, Inc.

The Invention of the Light Bulb

Map Study

Thomas Alva Edison invented the first incandescent light bulb that could be used in homes and offices. It was invented in his laboratory in Menlo Park, New Jersey, in 1882.

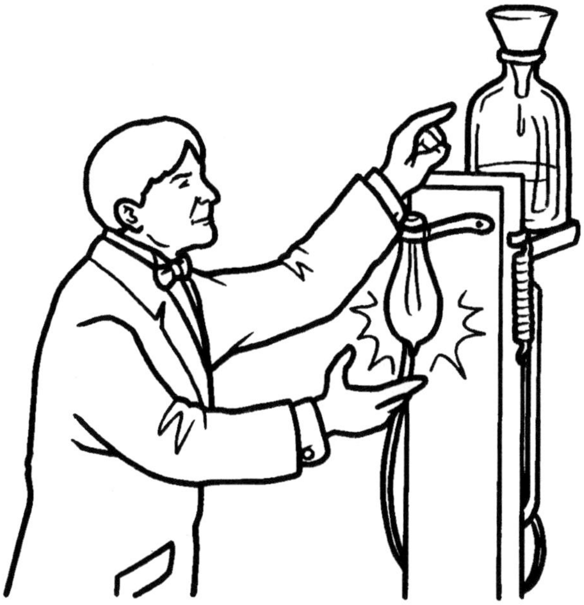

The Invention of

the Light Bulb

Cover page

Illustration for page 1

Glue

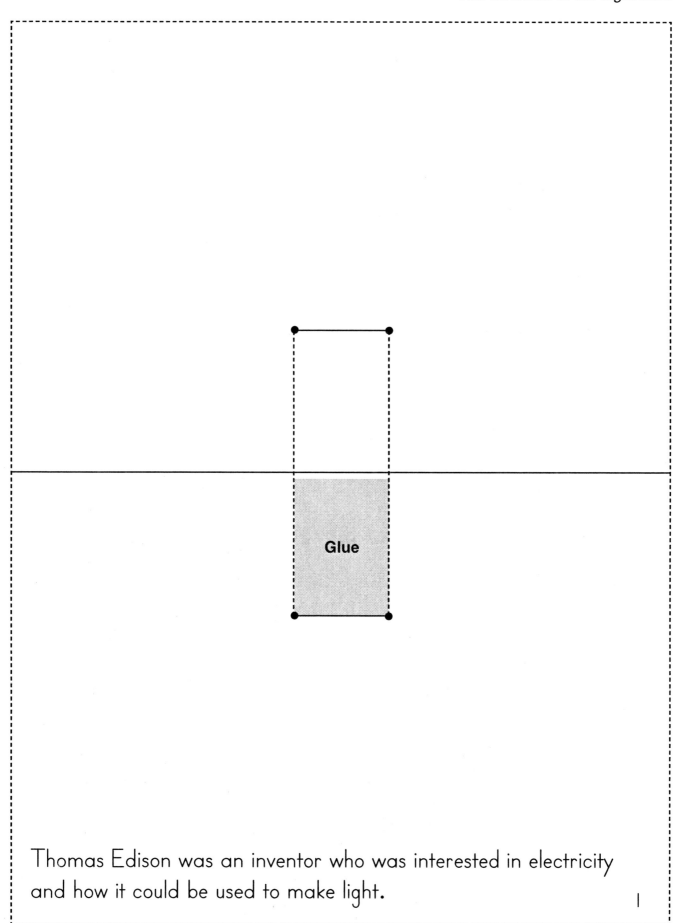

Thomas Edison was an inventor who was interested in electricity and how it could be used to make light.

1

Glue

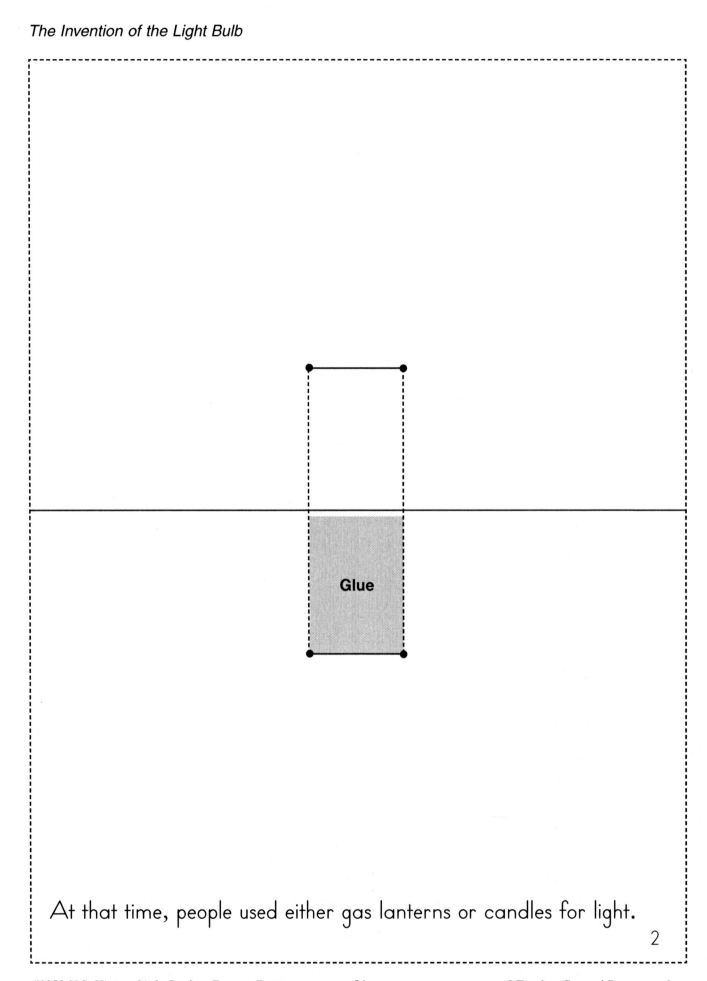

At that time, people used either gas lanterns or candles for light.

2

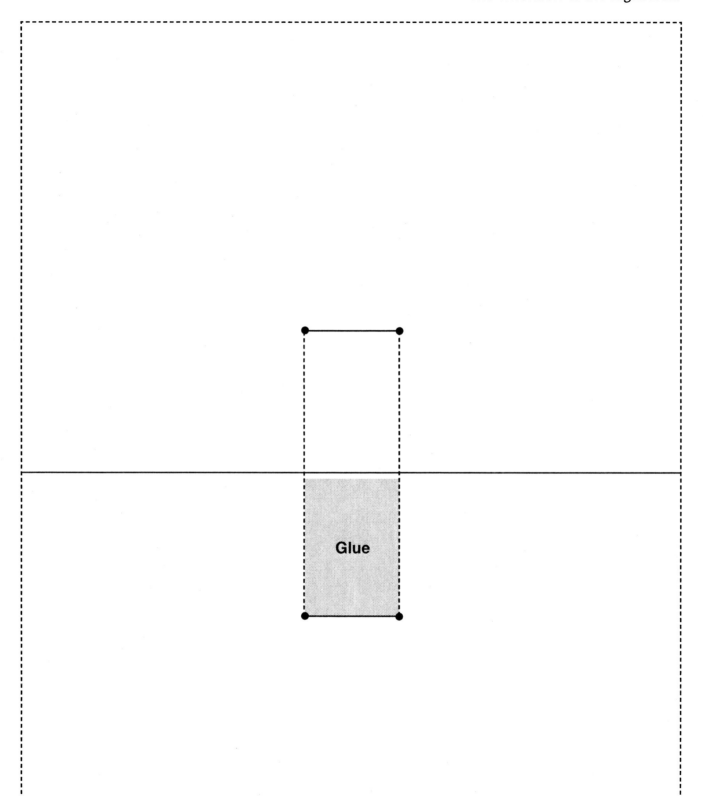

Glue

Mr. Edison made a glass bulb for the glow to show through and then tried many things to use as a wire or filament in the bulb, including the red hair of a man's beard.

3

Glue

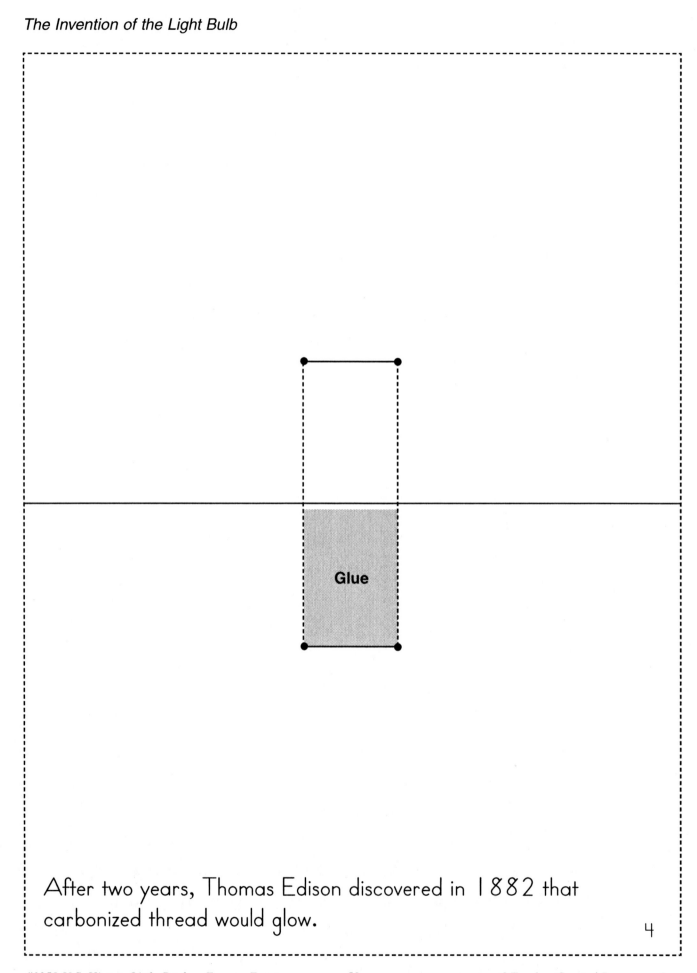

After two years, Thomas Edison discovered in 1882 that carbonized thread would glow.

4

Glue

Thomas Edison not only invented the electric light bulb but he also designed a power plant that made electricity more accessible to everyone in the world.

5

The Invention of the Light Bulb

Illustrations for pages 2 and 3

page 2

page 3

 ©Teacher Created Resources, Inc.

The Invention of the Light Bulb

Illustrations for pages 4 and 5

page 4

page 5

The Pony Express

From April 1860 to October 1861 the Pony Express was the fastest way to send mail 1,840 miles from St. Joseph, Missouri, to Sacramento, California. It served its purpose well for the short 18 months that it was needed. Ten-day mail delivery by way of the Pony Express was introduced as a better alternative to stagecoach delivery, which took as long as three weeks. The nation was on the brink of war, and the people of California and Oregon needed to be informed about issues as soon as possible.

The idea of using ponies to relay mail came from William H. Russell. He, Alexander Majors, and William B. Waddell were already heavily into the business of delivering army supplies out West and were hoping to get a contract for mail delivery as well. They promised delivery in 10 days at a cost of $5.00 per half-ounce, later reduced to $1.00 per half-ounce.

To begin, Russell, Majors, and Waddell secured about 420 high-grade broncos, thoroughbreds, mustangs, pintos, and Morgans and hired about 80 male riders. The riders ranged in age from 11 to 45 and weighed 110–125 lbs. The riders needed to be brave, expert gun handlers, excellent horsemen, and familiar with the fighting habits of Native Americans.

Russell and his men also hired 400 station men and women. One hundred and ninety stations were opened 15–25 miles apart, and horses and station keepers were placed at each station. The riders would race at the top speed of about 10 miles per hour from one "relay station" to the next where they would make two-minute switches to fresh horses, then continue on. Specially designed mail-filled saddlebags called mochilas were easily transferred from one horse to another. Riders rode about 75 miles at a stretch before stopping at what was called a "home station." At the home station they would dismount and send a new pony and mail carrier on for another 75 miles.

The first rider headed west from St. Joseph on April 3, 1860. His name was Johnnie Frye. Amidst enthusiastic ceremony, he galloped away at the sound of cannonball fire. He carried about 80 letters, including one of congratulations from President Buchanan to the Governor of California. He ferried across the Missouri River, then took the first leg of the trip on the old Oregon Trail. The first eastbound rider was Sam Hamilton. Saddled with mail that had come via steamboat (the *Antelope*) from San Francisco, his first stretch from Sacramento was rainy, muddy, cold, and hazardous. But, within the promised 10 days, mail reached both east and west destinations. The riders were warmly received as the crowds cheered and celebrations ensued.

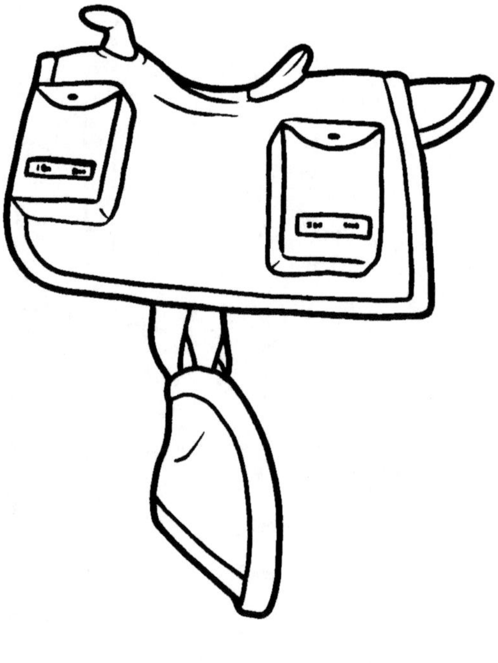

 ©Teacher Created Resources, Inc.

The Pony Express *(cont.)*

The most famous Pony Express rider was William F. Cody, known as Buffalo Bill. He began on the Pony Express as a substitute and was later hired full time. He had worked for the owners' freight company. One time he arrived at a relay station to find that a rider had been attacked and killed. He took the mail another leg, picked up the mail there and returned home, breaking a record of an amazing 384 miles ridden without a sleep break!

A speed record was broken when delivering President Abraham Lincoln's inaugural address to California in seven days and seventeen hours. On one of the legs of that trip, rider Bob Haslam, known as "Pony Bob," pushed his speed to an incredible 15 miles per hour! He was able to travel this fast while enduring the pain of a broken jaw from an arrow and a hurt arm from gunshot wounds.

As exciting as it was, the Pony Express was not bound to last forever. Poor business deals made by William Russell, the start of the Civil War, and the completion of the telegraph and transcontinental railroad all combined to cause its demise. In November of 1861, the Pony Express made its final delivery. While in existence though, in a total of 308 runs, riders had traveled 616,000 miles and delivered 34,753 pieces of mail. The entire time, only one mochila was lost.

The Pony Express represents the imagination, strength, and determination of the American people during the rapid growth of our nation in the mid-nineteenth century.

The Pony Express

Map Study

The Pony Express delivered mail from St. Joseph, Missouri, to Sacramento, California.

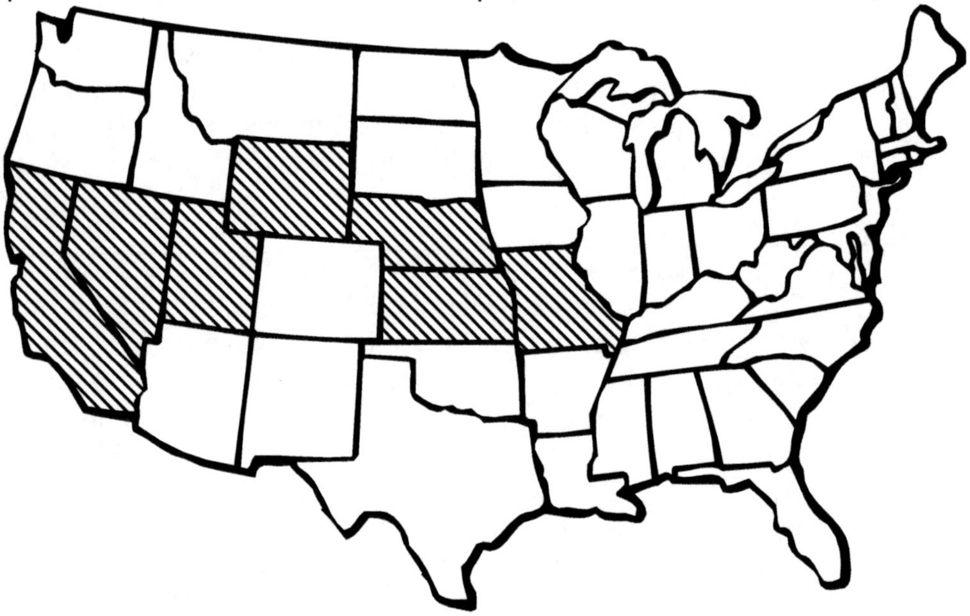

Trace the path the rider took through the territories between April 1860 and October 1861.

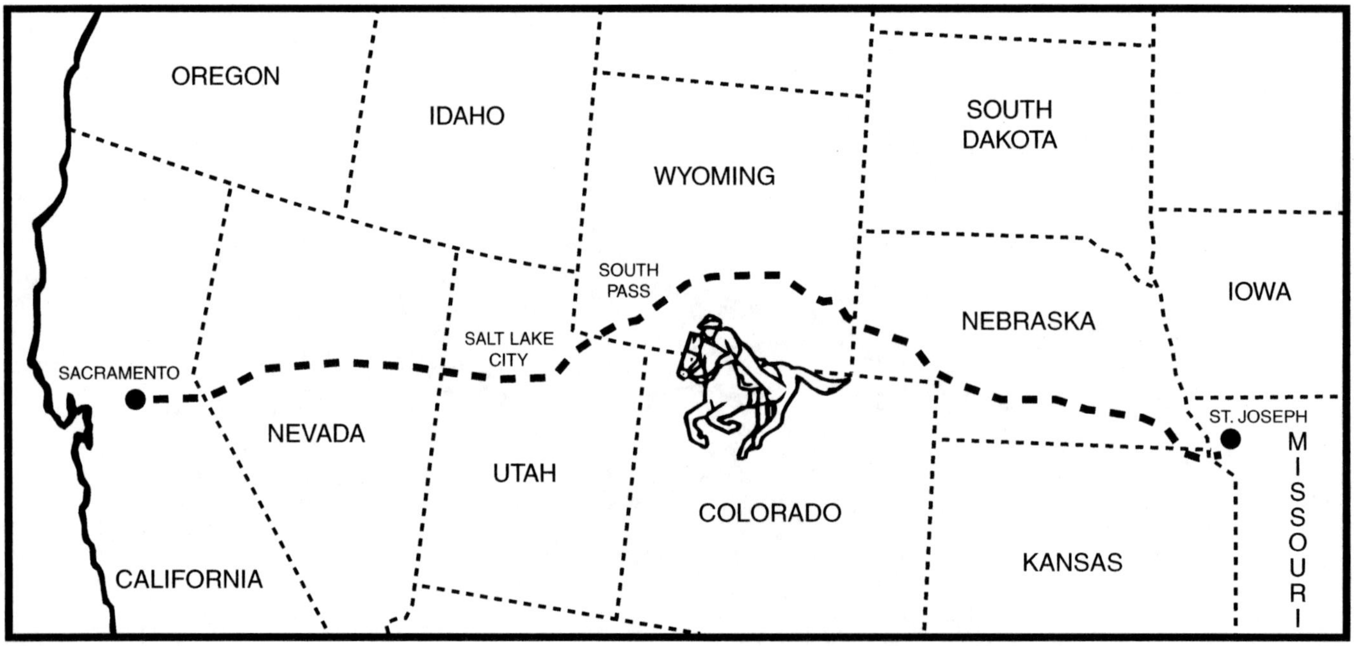

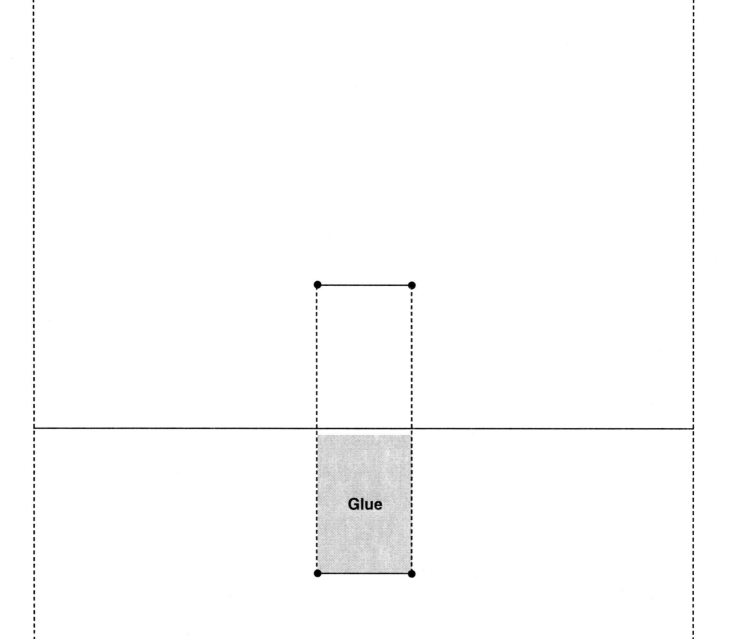

Glue

William H. Russell, Alexander Majors, and William B. Waddell introduced the Pony Express as a way to deliver mail from St. Joseph, Missouri, to Sacramento, California. They promised delivery in 10 days at a cost of $5 per half ounce. 1

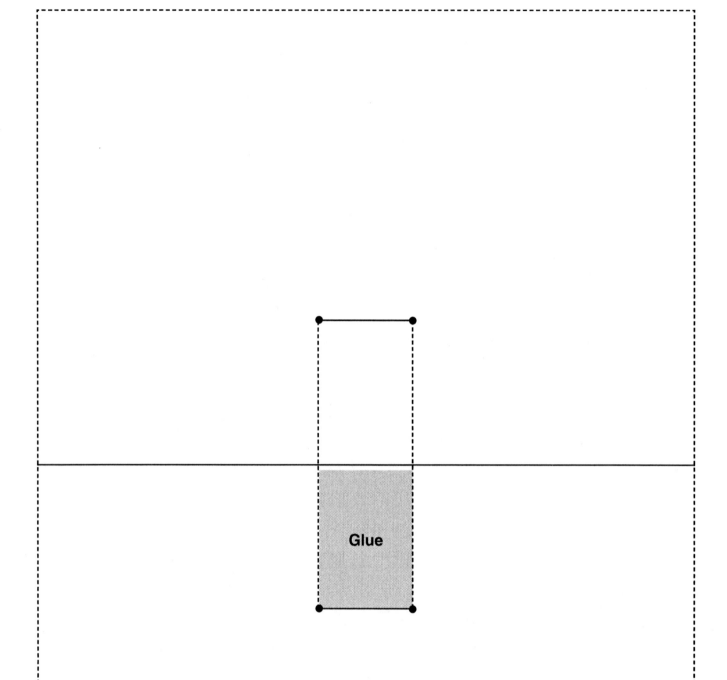

Glue

They secured about 420 high-grade ponies and about 80 male riders. Russell and his men also hired 400 station men and women. One hundred and ninety stations were opened 15–25 miles apart.

2

 ©Teacher Created Resources, Inc.

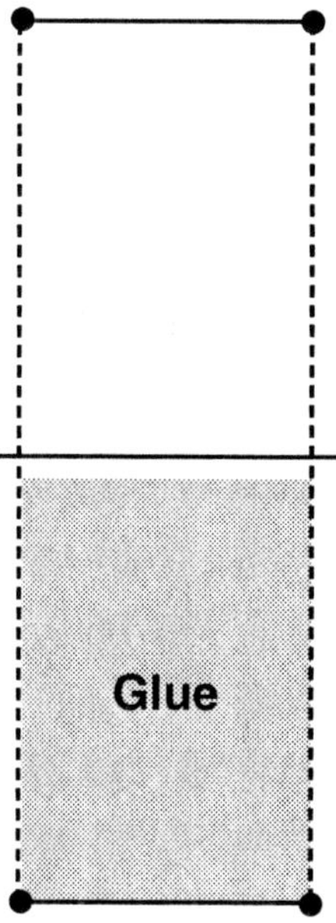

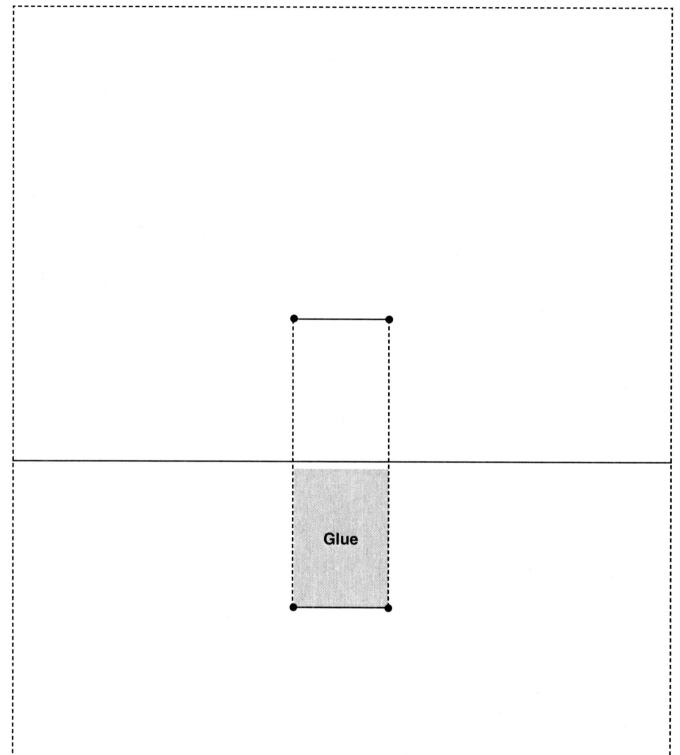

The riders would race at a top speed of about 10 miles per hour from one "relay station" to the next where they would make two-minute switches to fresh horses and continue on. Specially designed mail-filled saddlebags called mochilas were easily transferred from one horse to another. 3

Glue

The first riders departed on April 3, 1860. Though the trips were rough, the mail arrived ten days later and great celebrations took place.

4

Glue

The most famous Pony Express rider was William F. Cody, better known as Buffalo Bill. He made one 384-mile trip without stopping for a sleep break!

5

Glue

Rider Bob Haslam, known as "Pony Bob," pushed his speed to an incredible 15 miles per hour, doing his part to deliver President Abraham Lincoln's inaugural address to California. The whole trip was made in seven days and 17 hours.

6

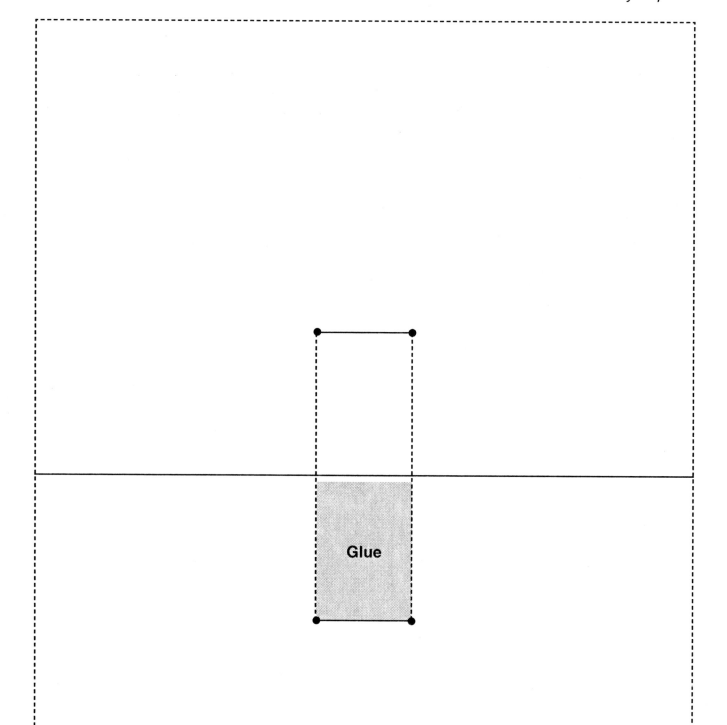

Glue

In November of 1861, the Pony Express made its final delivery. In a total of 308 runs, riders had traveled 616,000 miles and delivered 34,753 pieces of mail. The entire time, only one mochila was lost.

7

©Teacher Created Resources, Inc.

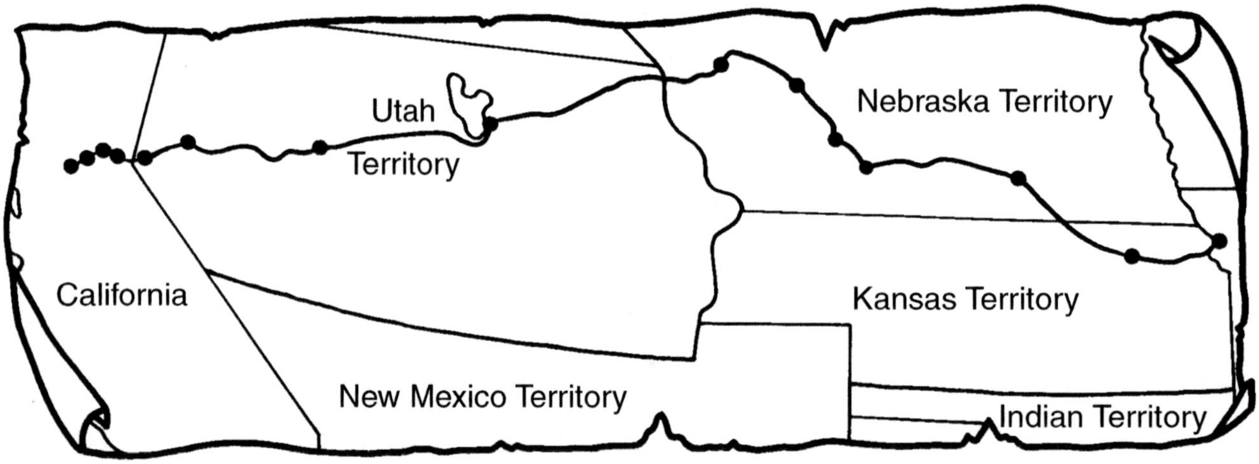

The Pony Express

Cover page

Illustrations for pages 1 and 3.

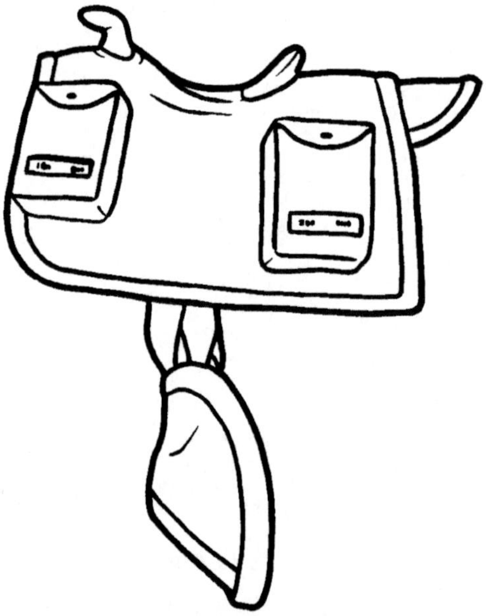

page 3

page 1

Pony Express Illustrations *(cont.)*

Illustrations for pages 2 and 4

page 2

page 4

Pony Express Illustrations *(cont.)*

Illustrations for pages 5, 6, and 7

William F. Cody

page 5

"Pony Bob"

page 6

NOTICE

BY ORDERS FROM THE EAST,

THE PONY EXPRESS

WILL be DISCONTINUED.

The Last Pony coming this way left Atchison, Kansas, yesterday.

WELLS, FARGO & CO., Agents

page 7

 ©Teacher Created Resources, Inc.

The California Gold Rush

A man named John Sutter owned some land in California. He hired some men to build a sawmill on the land. The foreman on the job, John W. Marshal, saw flecks of gold sparkling in the millrace and pointed them out to Mr. Sutter. Within a month, the news had spread about the discovery of gold in the American River in California.

In 1849, thousands of people rushed to California hoping to get rich mining for gold. They became known as "forty-niners." The first difficulty for the "forty-niners" was how to get to California. Some traveled on a ship from the east coast all the way around South America. Others seeking gold took a ship to Mexico or Panama, crossed the land, and then boarded another ship and traveled up the coastline to California. Most people, however, made the journey west in wagons or by horseback.

After taking the perilous trip, the "forty-niners" discovered that everything was very expensive near the gold fields. People were so busy trying to strike it rich that they did not take the time to build permanent lodging or take care of sanitation needs. There were no good places to live, and diseases such as cholera were spreading. People also found that gold mining was very, very tedious work. There were different methods for "mining." Panning for gold or scooping up dirt in a stream was the fastest way to get started. A cradle and a trough could also be used to extract the gold. These worked on the same principle as the pan in that the dirt was put into the cradle or trough; water was then poured over the dirt and the heavier gold would go to the bottom. Other miners dug into the ground. Still others blasted the mountainside using strong sprays of water to get the gold. The hydraulic mining method (using water) was banned after 1884 because of the damage it caused to the environment.

The California Gold Rush *(cont.)*

There were no laws in the area when the Gold Rush began. People would argue over land claims or try to cheat each other by saying there was gold on land by planting a gold nugget on it.

Not many people became rich from the gold but a lot of people became rich by furnishing supplies to the gold diggers. A man named Philip Armour sold beef to the miners from his butcher shop. This is a familiar name on such things as hot dogs today. Another man named Levi Strauss sold canvas for tents. He also had someone make pants out of a tough fabric dyed blue called denim so the miners would be able to be on their knees all day.

Because the miners needed entertaining, singers, dancers, and actors began their careers in the area. "Oh Susanna," written by Steven Foster, was performed so often that it became a popular folk song and an inspiration for the miners. To this day, entertainment is a major industry in California.

The California Gold Rush only lasted a few years, but the negative effects of it were significant. Mining caused major environmental changes. The land was mutilated by miners in a hurry to find gold. Plants were unable to grow and animals were unable to survive without vegetation for food and shelter. Pollution was also evident.

As miners and the people working the businesses increased in population, Native Americans lost their land and their homes. Diseases brought by the settlers and the miners caused many of the Native Americans to die.

Gold mining led to the mining of natural resources such as coal, oil, salt, copper, and tin. The population of California grew quickly because so many people had moved to the area to seek their fortunes. California grew so fast that it became a state in 1850, only two years after the discovery of gold at Sutter's Mill.

The California Gold Rush

Map Study

The California Gold Rush began on the American River near Sacramento, California.

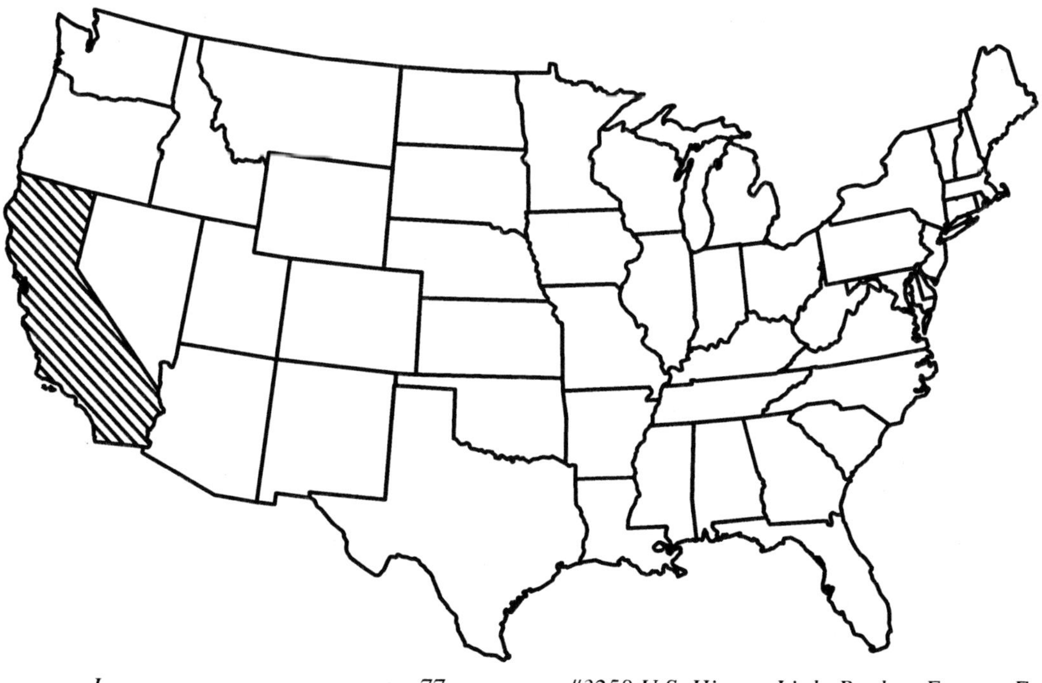

Putting Together
The California Gold Rush

Materials

Each student will need:

- one sheet each of dark blue, tan, and dark brown construction paper
- two sheets of light blue construction paper
- gold or yellow scraps of paper cut in the shape of gold nuggets
- copies of text, illustrations, and template pages (pages 79–82)
- scissors, glue, stapler, and crayons

Assembly Directions for the Layered Book

1. Cut out and color the illustrations.
2. Cut out the templates and trace them on the colored paper as directed.
   Note: Delete directions on the templates if color copies are made prior to the activity.
3. Cut the two pieces of light blue construction paper into 6½" x 9" rectangles.
4. Layer from back to front as follows: light blue, dark brown, tan, dark blue, and light blue cover.
5. Make sure the straight edges are even on the bottom and left sides.
6. Staple down the left side of the booklet.
7. Number the pages. Begin with number 1 on the inside front cover.
8. Glue the title and illustration to the cover.
9. Cut out the lines of text.
10. Glue the appropriate text strips to the pages.
11. Add a an extra strip of blue for the river on page 6. Add the illustrations to pages 6 and 8.
12. Glue gold "nuggets" on each page.

The California Gold Rush

Layered Book Text

Gold was discovered in California in 1848. Thousands of people travelled West to strike it rich. 1

The miners discovered that it was hard work mining for gold. The cost of food and lodging was expensive and living conditions were poor. 3

Most miners panned for gold in the riverbeds. Some tried to find gold by digging in the ground and in the mountainsides. 5

So many people moved to California during the Gold Rush that it became a state in 1850. Both the entertainment industry in California and the mining industry for the United States began during this time. 7

Illustrations for page 6

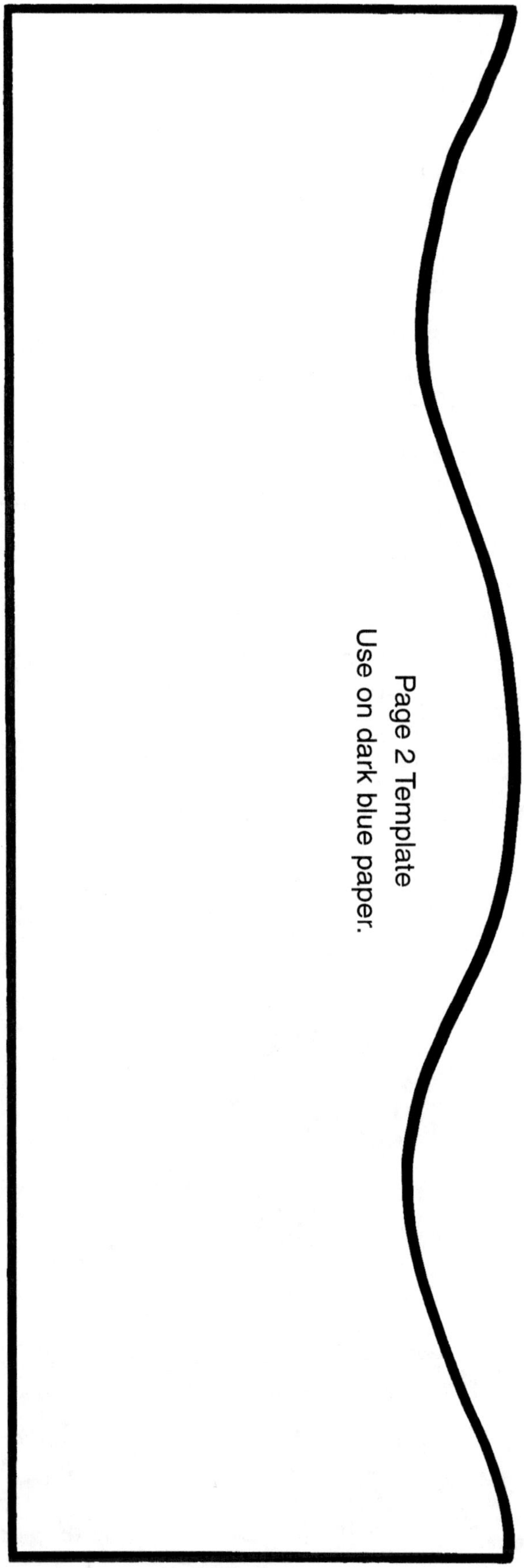
Page 2 Template
Use on dark blue paper.

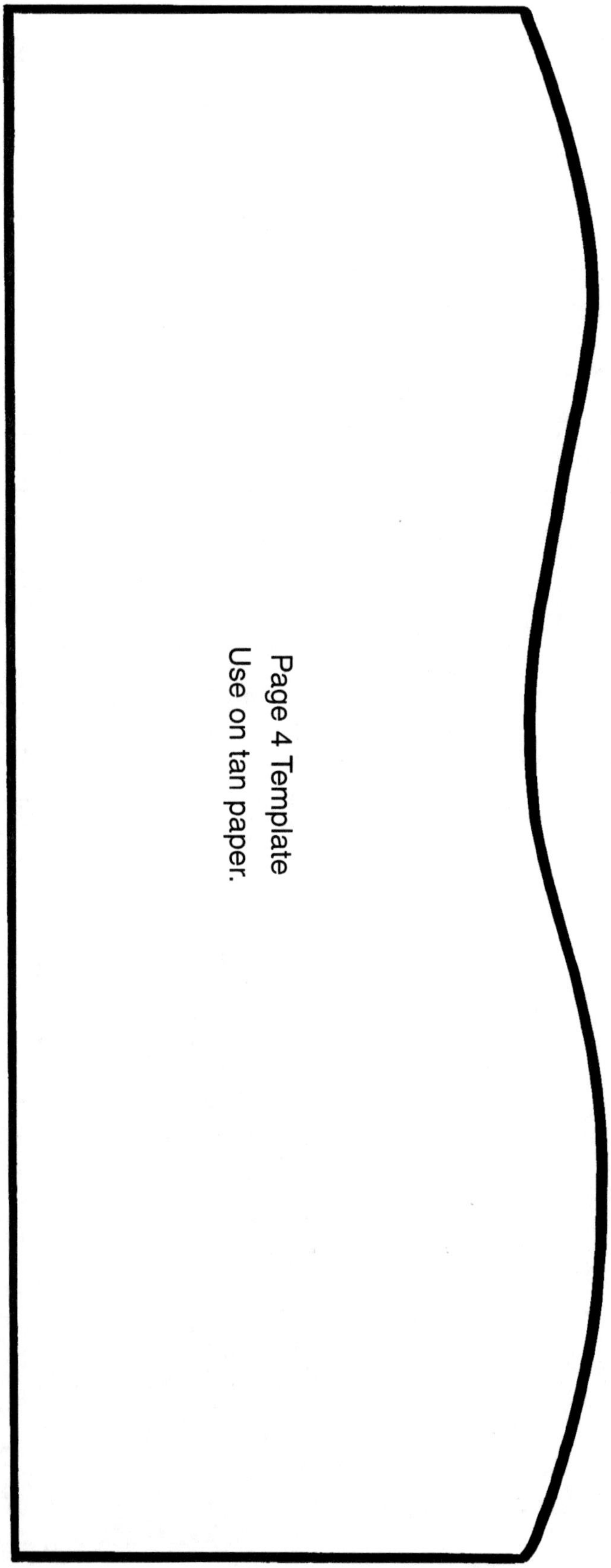
Page 4 Template
Use on tan paper.

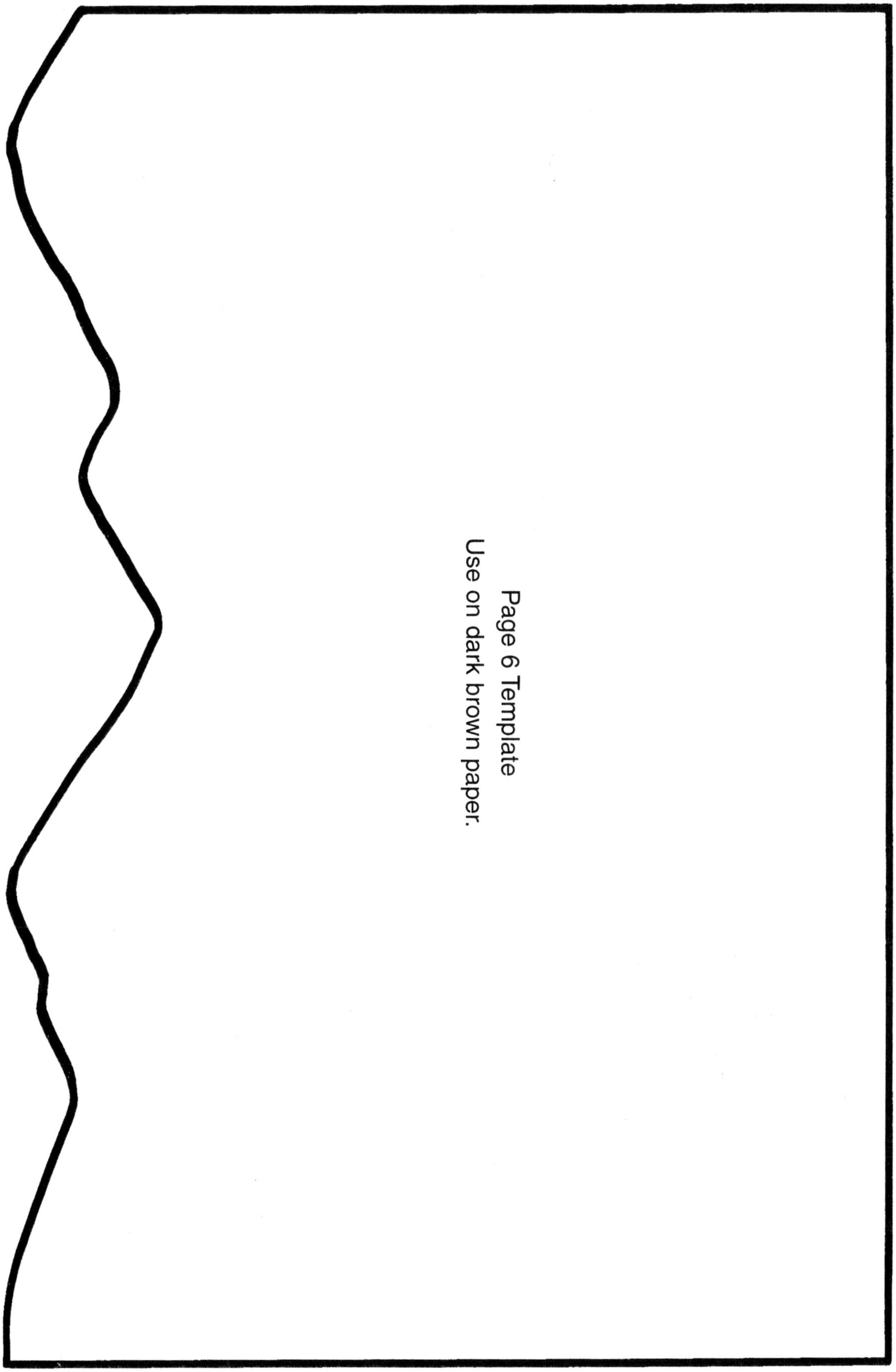
Page 6 Template
Use on dark brown paper.

The California Gold Rush

The California Gold Rush

Cover page

page 8

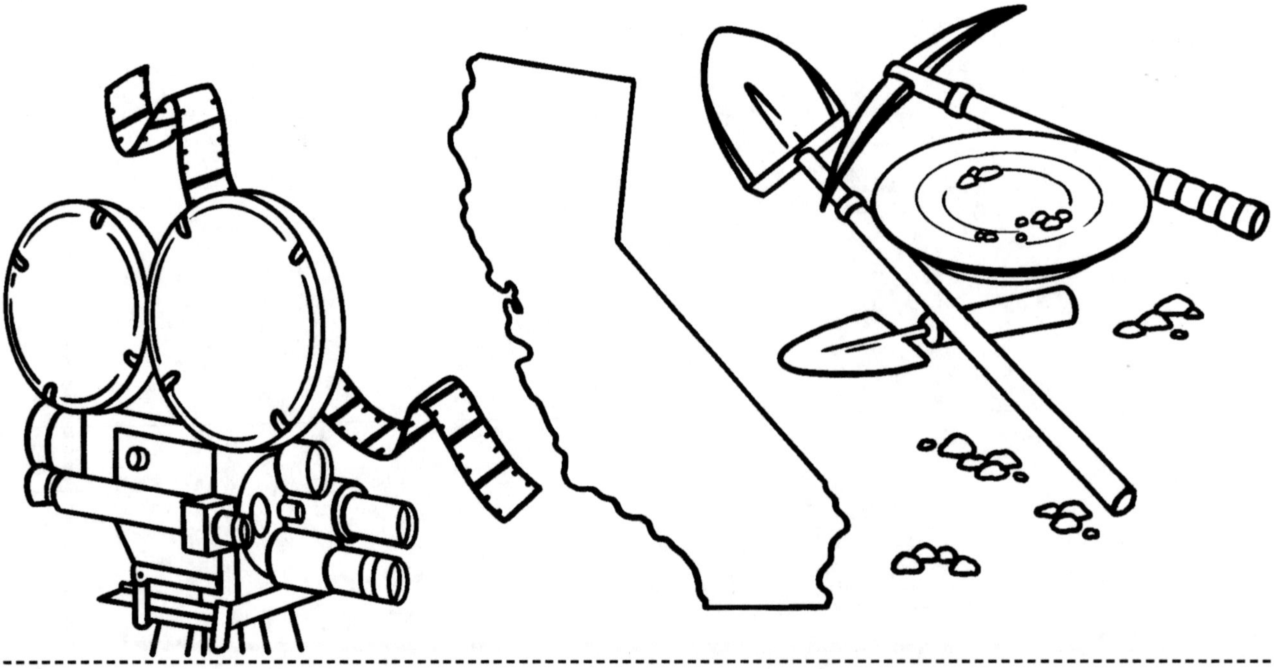

 ©Teacher Created Resources, Inc.

Transportation Firsts

Since the beginning of time, people have been interested in locomotion and how to transport human beings and goods from place to place. Transportation has been a fascinating subject since the invention of the wheel about 5,000 years ago. Consider some of the inventions of ancient civilizations (axle, pulley, wheel). Americans, too, have made great contributions in the transportation field.

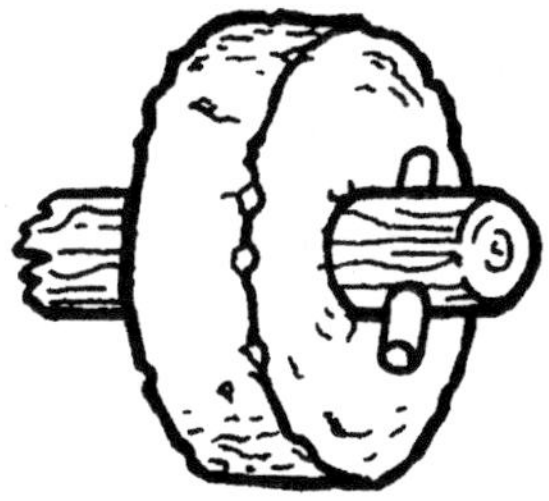

Native Americans used canoes formed by hollowing out logs. These canoes were heavy and slow. In 1787, a man named John Fitch built a steamboat. His boat had large paddles on the sides and moved by a steam engine. He transported people on the Delaware River, but because the engine was so large, there wasn't room for many people. As a result, his business failed.

In 1804, another American named John Stevens invented a steamboat that was able to go the speed of eight knots. His *Phoenix* became the first steamboat to take a sea voyage from New York to Philadelphia. In 1807, Robert Fulton had the first successful steamboat service on the Hudson River. His boat, the *Clermont*, could carry 24 people at a time, and goods. This steamboat had a paddlewheel instead of individual paddles. By 1846, there were approximately 1,200 steamboats on the rivers, transporting people and materials. River commerce became very important to the United States.

In 1830, the Baltimore and Ohio Railroad began the first steam-operated railway service to carry passengers in the United States. The first train car was actually a "car" pulled by a horse. The railroad began in Baltimore. Service did not get to Ohio until 1863.

Charleston, South Carolina, had the first railway service using steam locomotives. The engineering faculty at the United States Military Academy in West Point, New York, was instrumental in building this locomotive, or steam-engine car. *The Best Friend of Charleston* was shipped to Charleston. There, in 1830, it pulled a train of cars for six miles.

Railroads linked the two oceans in the United States, the Atlantic and Pacific. Modern locomotives are diesel-electric and are used mostly to transport goods instead of human beings.

Transportation Firsts *(cont.)*

There is a lot of confusion over the invention of the "horseless carriage," known as the automobile in the United States. George B. Selden got a patent for the automobile in 1879. He kept it pending for 16 years, disallowing others from claiming the invention. Some say that Charles and Frank Duryea were responsible for the first gasoline automobiles in the United States. In 1895, Frank Duryea won the first car race with more than two participating cars. Others say that John William Lambert of Ohio invented the first gas-powered, single-cylinder car. Automobiles were not well received initially because they were very loud and the noise scared horses and people. Also, they were a threat to the railroad and stagecoach businesses.

Automobiles were essentially made only for the rich until Henry Ford started mass-producing Model T's in 1908. He put workers on an assembly line. Each person had one specific job to do in creating the car. Cars were made more cheaply and quickly after this. Road mileage first became greater than rail mileage in 1915, and the difference has continued to grow.

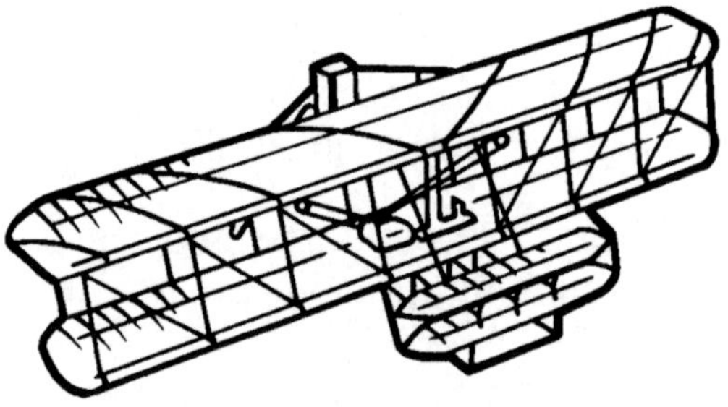

Wilbur and Orville Wright were not engineers. They didn't even complete high school. They owned a bicycle shop in Dayton, Ohio. They became interested in flying. They left Dayton during the bicycle shop off-season and set up a tent at Kitty Hawk, North Carolina. They were told by the weather bureau that Kitty Hawk was a very windy location and had high sand dunes.

On December 17, 1903, Orville Wright became the first man to take an airplane ride on the *Flyer*. The plane was made of wood, wire, and cloth. The plane had a gasoline engine. The pilot had to lie down in the middle and as he moved his hips, a wire attached from his waist to the wings would control the balance of the wings. Very little news came out about this flight, and at the time people did not seem to be interested.

Air travel has since become the fastest means of transportation in the world.

 ©Teacher Created Resources, Inc.

Transportation Firsts

Map Study

Transportation Firsts: Where They All Began

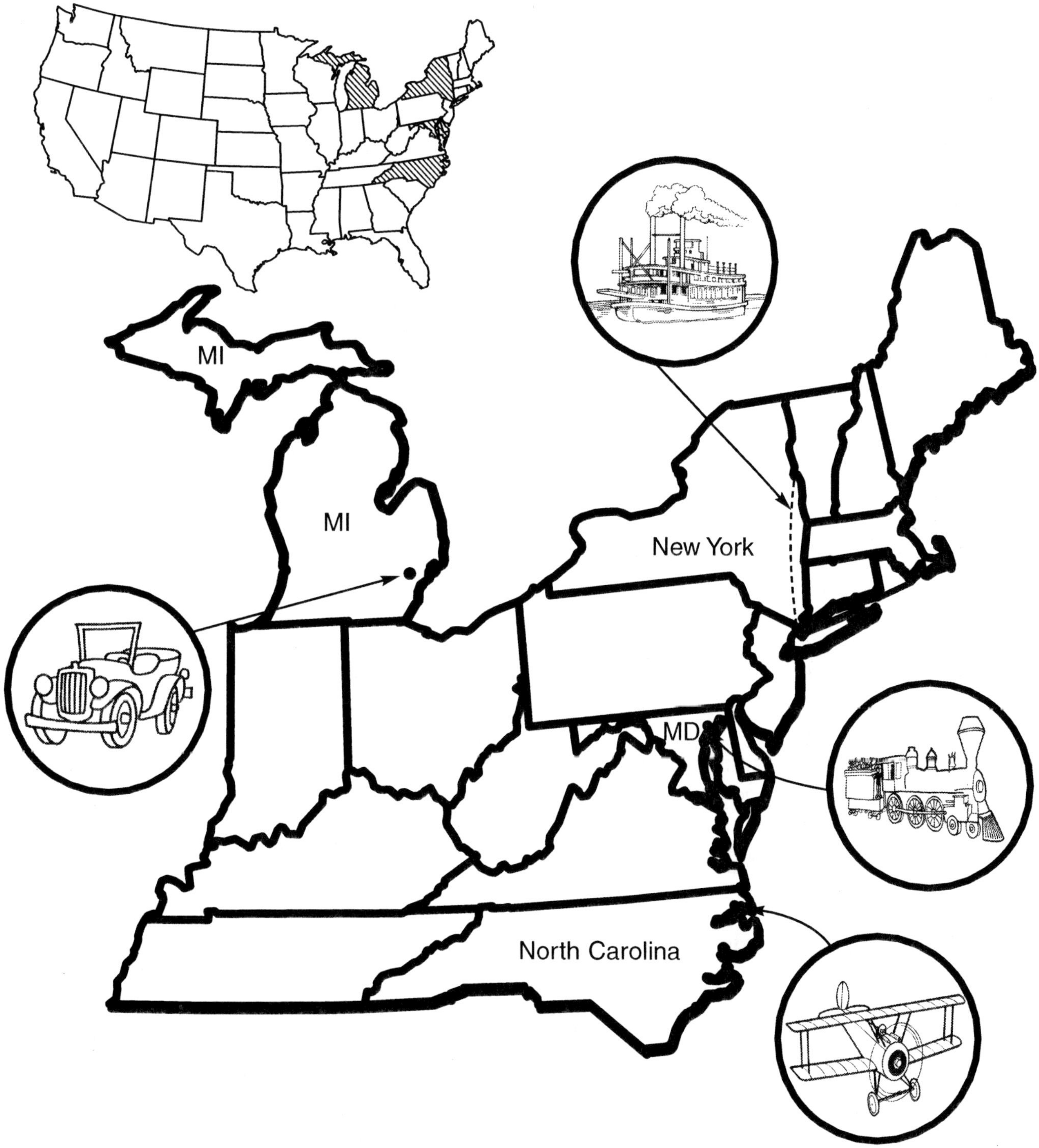

Putting Together *Transportation Firsts*

Materials

For each student you will need:

- one sheet each of dark blue, green, and dark brown construction paper
- two sheets of 9" x 6" light blue construction paper
- copies of text, illustrations, and template pages (pages 87–93)
- scissors, glue, crayons, and stapler

Assembly Directions for the Layered Book

1. Color the illustrations.
2. Cut out the templates.
3. Trace the templates onto the appropriate color of construction paper. **Note:** Delete directions on the template if color copies are to be made prior to the activity.
4. Cut out the construction paper pages as directed on the templates.
5. Attach (glue) the smaller brown piece to the bottom of the green piece to form the road for the car.
6. Layer from back to front as follows: light blue, brown/green, brown, dark blue, and the light-blue cover.
7. Make sure the straight edges are even on the bottom and left sides. Staple down the left side of the booklet. Number the book pages, beginning with the inside cover.
8. Cut out the text strips and the illustrations.
9. Glue the appropriate illustration to the page. Be sure that it will be hidden under the preceding pages. (Because the book unfolds in layers, you do not want the illustrations to interfere with one another.)
10. Glue the appropriate text in the center of the page opposite the illustration, beginning with the back of the cover (page 1).

 ©Teacher Created Resources, Inc.

Transportation Firsts

Layered Book Text

Robert Fulton's *Clermont* became the first successful steamboat service in the United States.

1

In 1830, the Baltimore and Ohio Railroad began the first railway service in the United States. It used a car pulled by a horse. Charleston, South Carolina, had the first railway service using steam locomotives.

3

Automobiles were made only for the rich until Henry Ford started mass-producing Model T's in 1908.

5

In 1903, Wilbur and Orville Wright were responsible for the first successful airplane flight. The flight took place at Kitty Hawk, North Carolina.

7

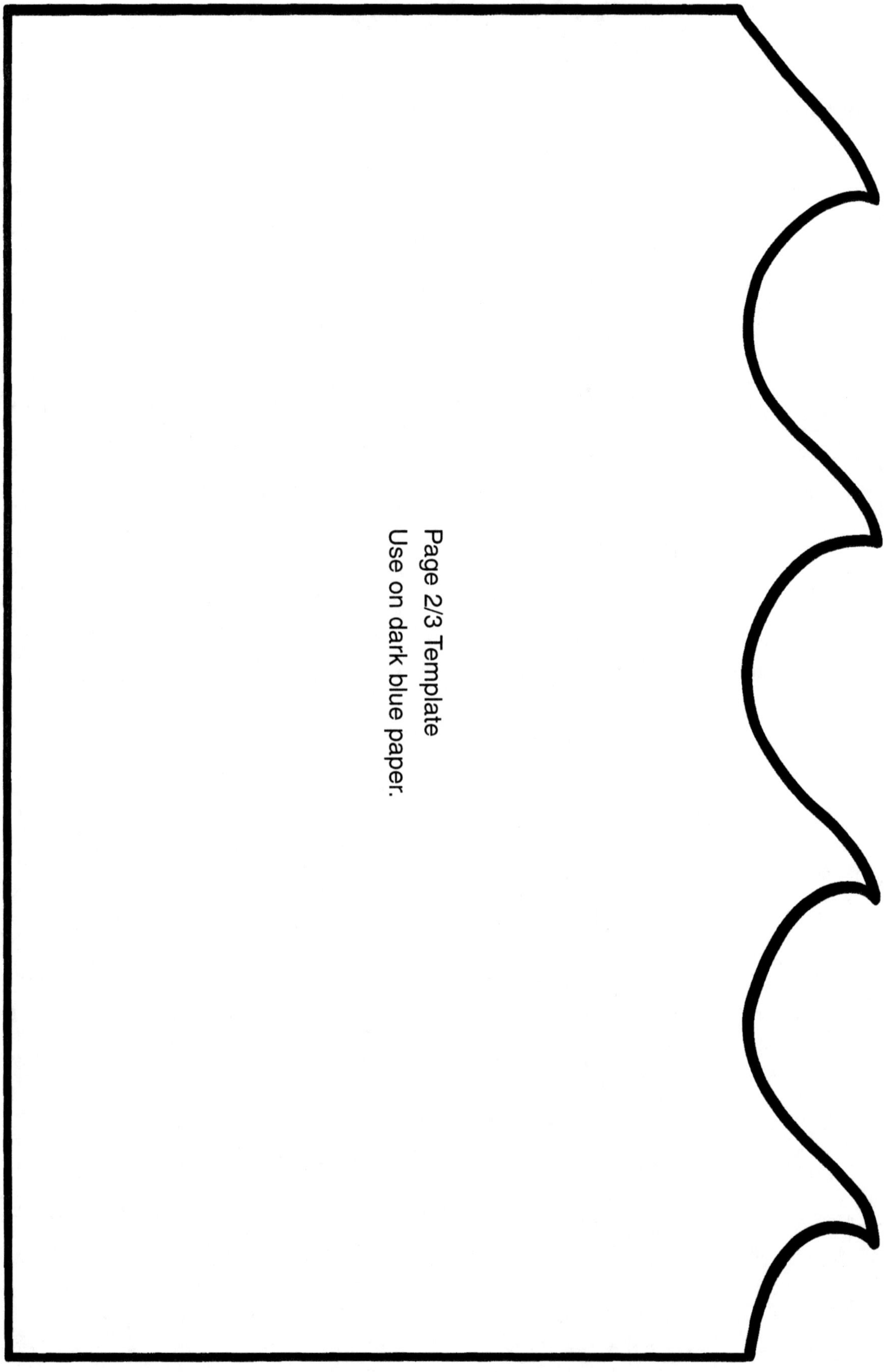
Page 2/3 Template
Use on dark blue paper.

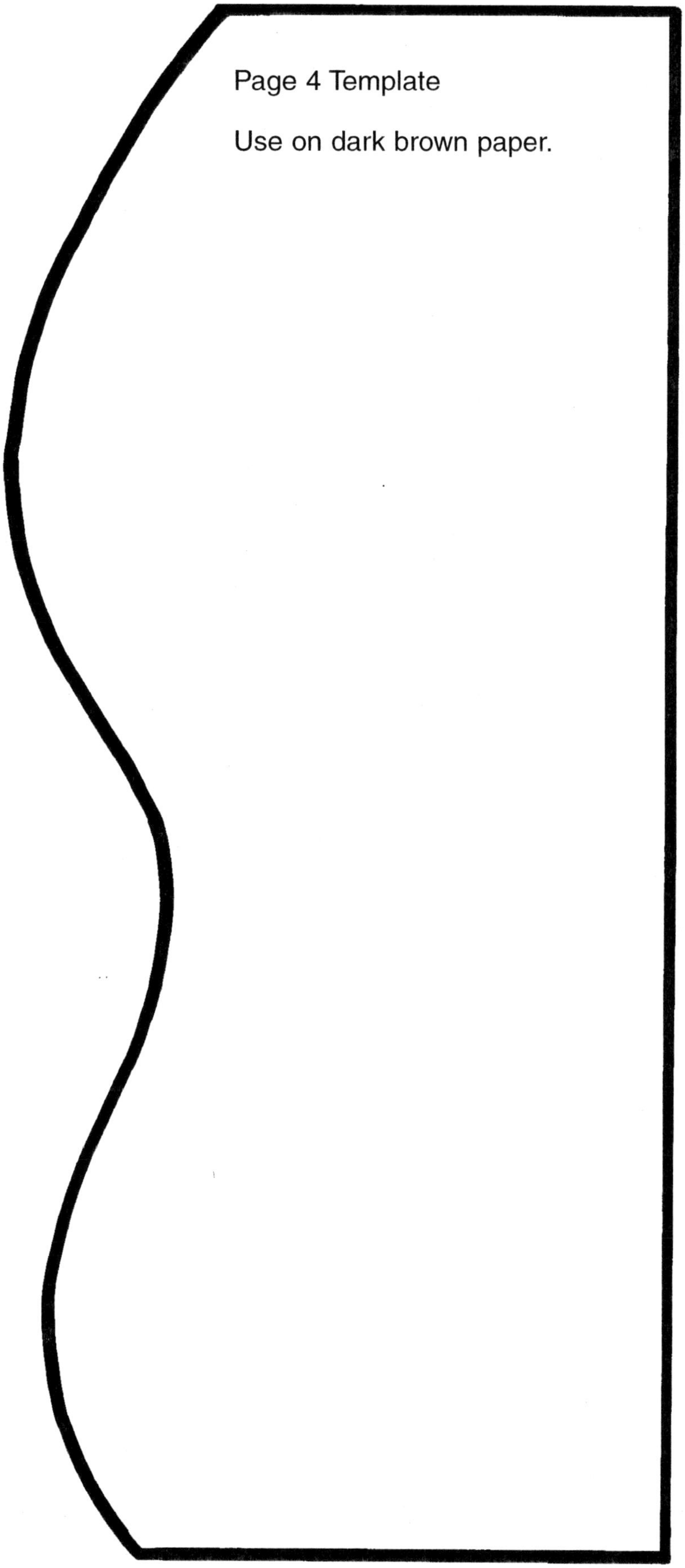
Page 4 Template
Use on dark brown paper.

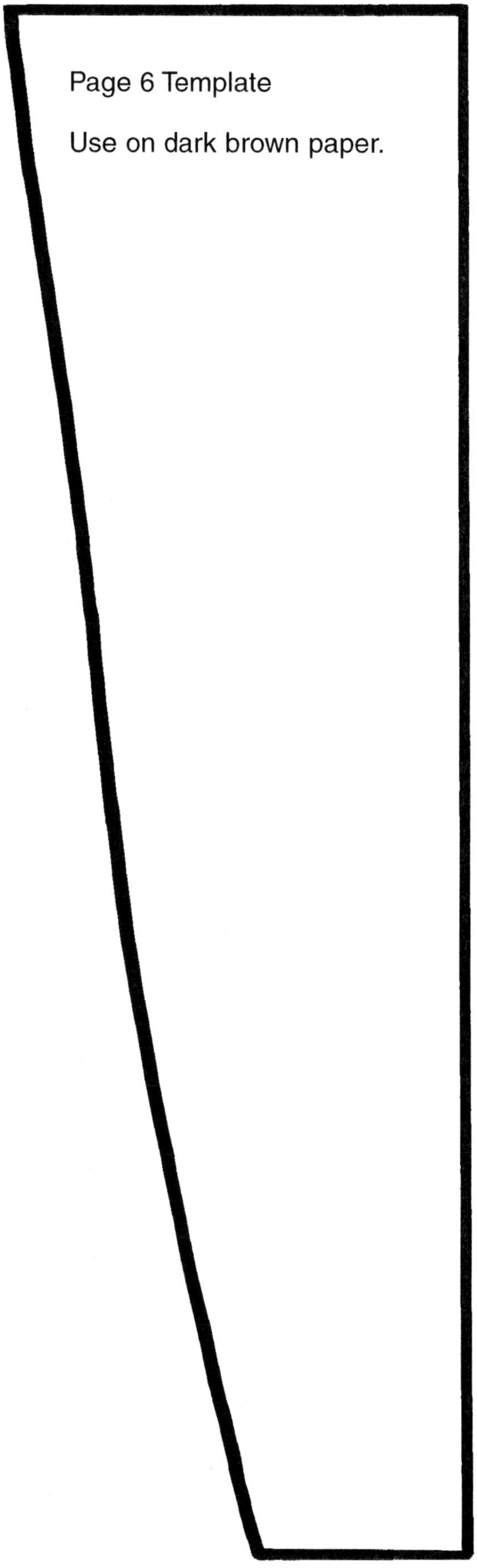
Page 6 Template
Use on dark brown paper.

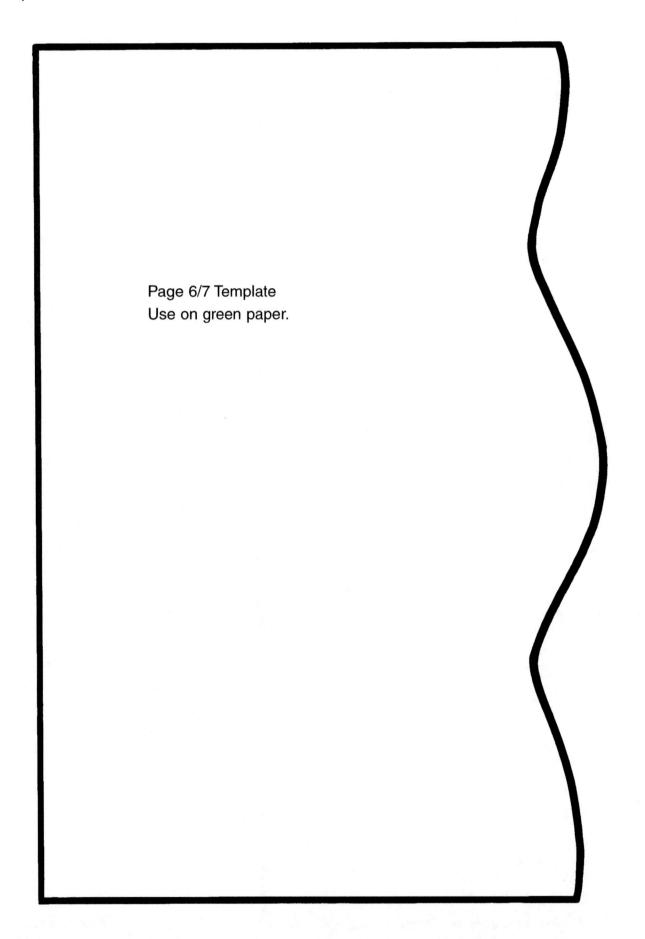

Page 6/7 Template
Use on green paper.

©Teacher Created Resources, Inc.

Transportation Firsts

Illustration for page 2

Steamboat

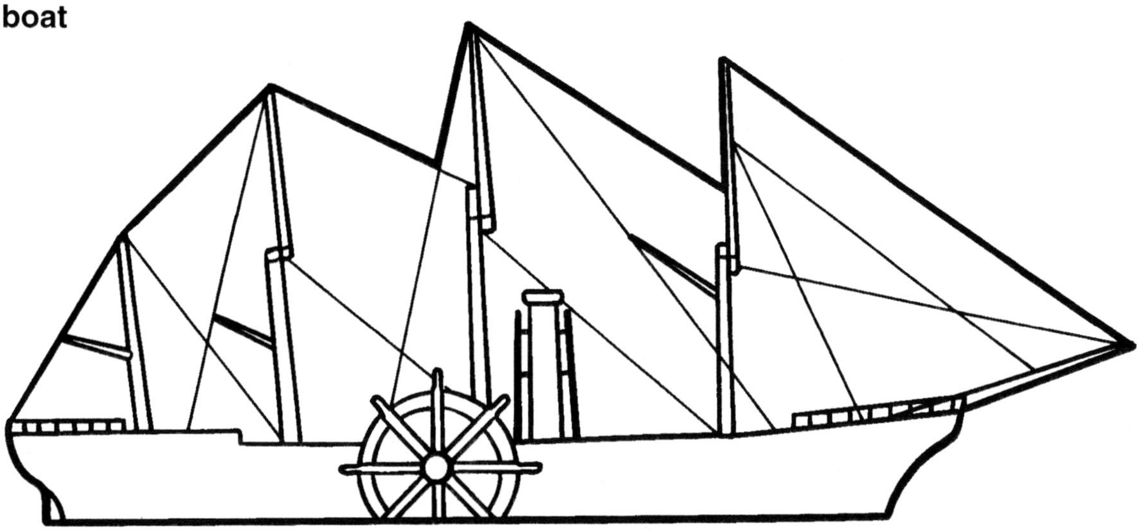

Cover Page

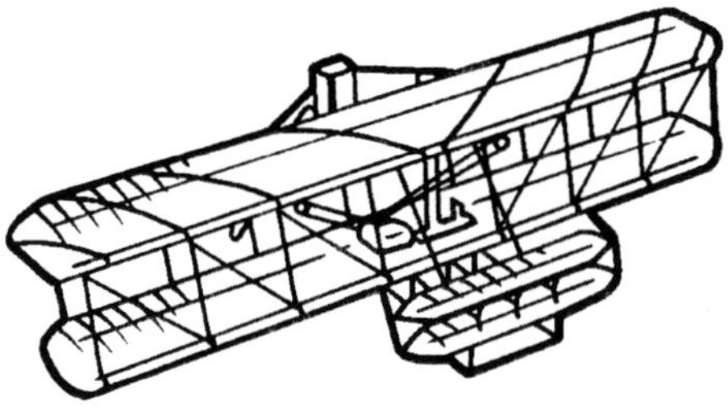

Transportation Firsts

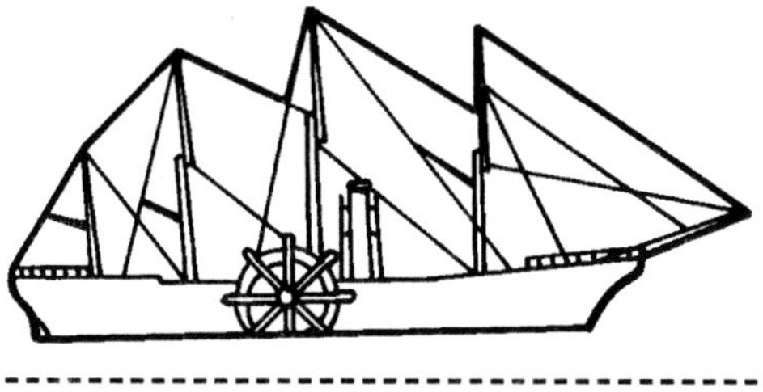

Transportation Firsts

Illustrations for pages 4 and 6

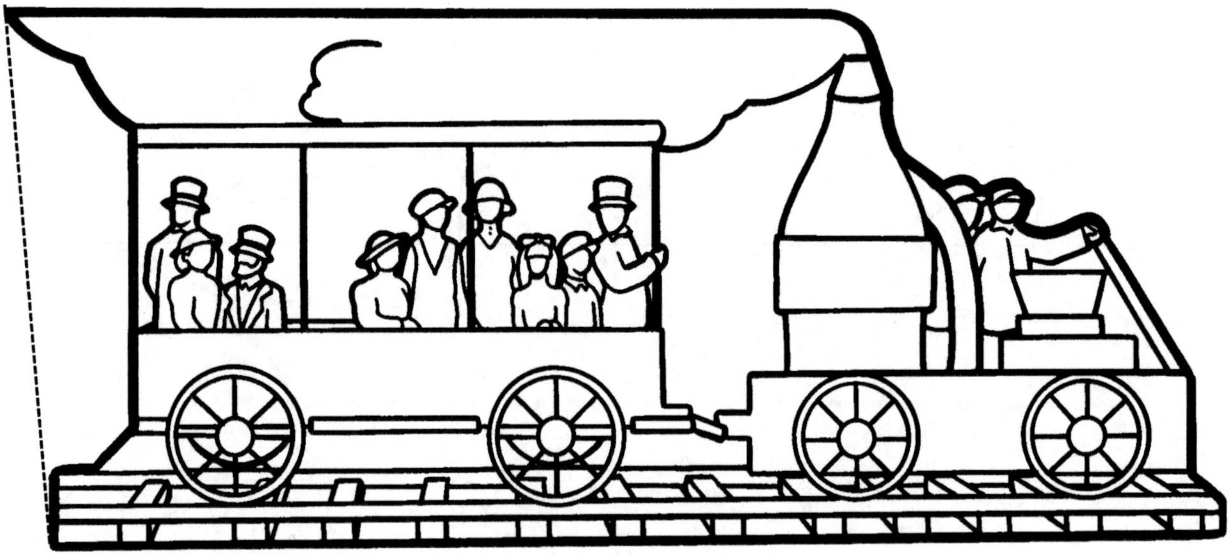

Steam Locomotive

Model T Car

 ©Teacher Created Resources, Inc.

Transportation Firsts

Illustration for page 8

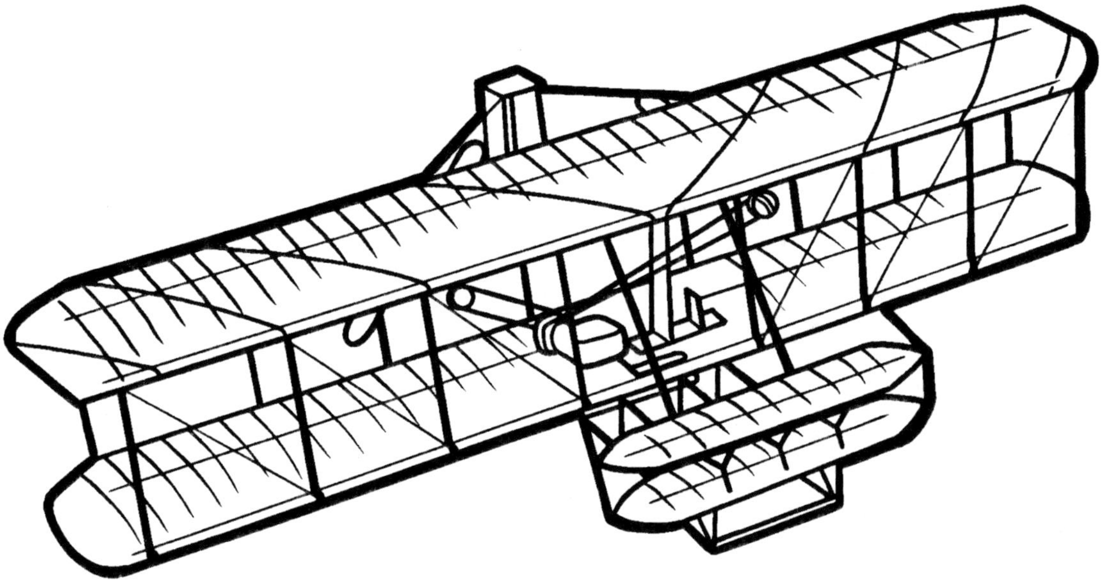

Airplane

The Growth of the U.S.A.

The borders of the United States of America changed drastically between the years 1783 and 1959. The nation expanded at a tremendous rate, inspired by proud people who were industrious and enthusiastic.

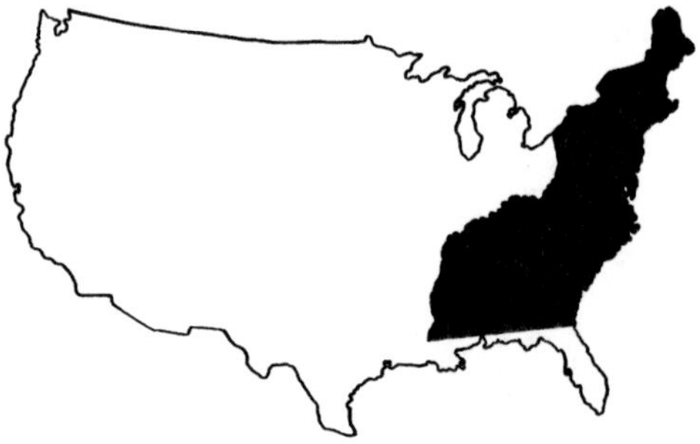

The colonists won the Revolutionary War against Great Britain, proving themselves to be an independent, sovereign nation. The Treaty of Paris was signed, declaring that the 13 colonies would be recognized as the United States of America. Along with the colonies, the Americans acquired the land that extended west to the Mississippi River, except for what is now Florida. That land was Spanish territory.

In 1787 after the U.S. Constitution was written, the Northwest Ordinance was passed. From that, the Northwest Territory was established. Ohio, Indiana, Illinois, Michigan, Wisconsin, and part of Minnesota were later created from this area. Spain, Great Britain, and France all had interests in the land to the west of the existing United States and the Northwest Territory. Louisiana, the land between the Mississippi River and the Rocky Mountains was first controlled by France, then ceded to Spain in 1762. Louisiana was secretly given back to the French again in 1800. However, the French did not take possession in this last transaction.

In 1802, Spain essentially cut off American shipping privileges from the busy New Orleans port where the Americans traded. Spain did this by charging a high tax on all cargo that came through the port. President Thomas Jefferson sent some representatives to France in 1803 to negotiate the purchase of the city of New Orleans. The representatives discovered that the French ruler of that time, Napolean Bonaparte, was no longer interested in having a colony in that territory. He offered to sell them not only New Orleans, but all of Louisiana at the price of $15 million, roughly $4.00 per acre. The deal is touted today as one of the smoothest land transactions in history.

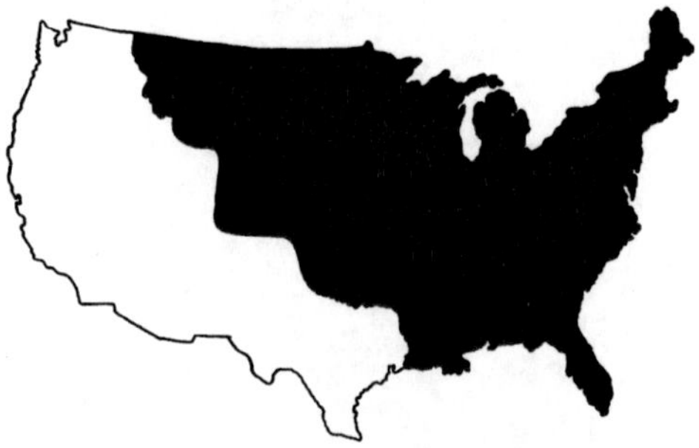

The United States had disagreements with both Great Britain and Spain over certain pockets of land. In 1818 they settled one issue over some land to the north. Great Britain agreed to the Red River Cession, which gave the U.S. the land between Louisiana on the west-side and the 49th parallel on the north. The same year, U.S. General Andrew Jackson invaded Florida in an attempt to take over. Spain signed over all of Florida to the U.S. by 1819.

The Growth of the U.S.A. *(cont.)*

The next area of expansion to the United States was the annexation of Texas. Once belonging to Mexico, Texas had become inhabited by more and more Americans until the number of Americans exceeded the number of Mexicans. At that point, the people of Texas revolted against Mexican rule and broke away, forming their own government. It was later that they wanted to become part of the United States. The year was 1845.

The following year, the United States expanded further west to the Pacific coast when they signed the Treaty of Guadalupe Hidalgo with Mexico and bought the land for 15 million dollars. Also in 1846, a joint occupation treaty between Great Britain and the United States expired. Great Britain gave the United States the Oregon Country, the land between the west coast of the Louisiana Purchase and the Pacific Ocean, just to the north of the land bought from Mexico.

The Gadsden Purchase of a portion of land just north of Mexico and west of Texas was made in 1853. This transaction made our continental United States complete.

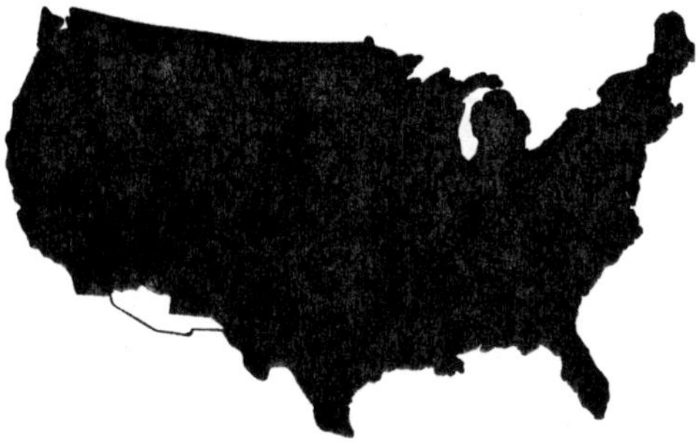

The United States bought the territory that is now Alaska from Russia in 1867. Hawaii was annexed by the United States in 1898. Over the years from 1783 to 1959, the U.S. territories became states, the last two being Alaska and Hawaii. The United States of America now consists of 50 states.

The Growth of the U.S.A.

Map Study

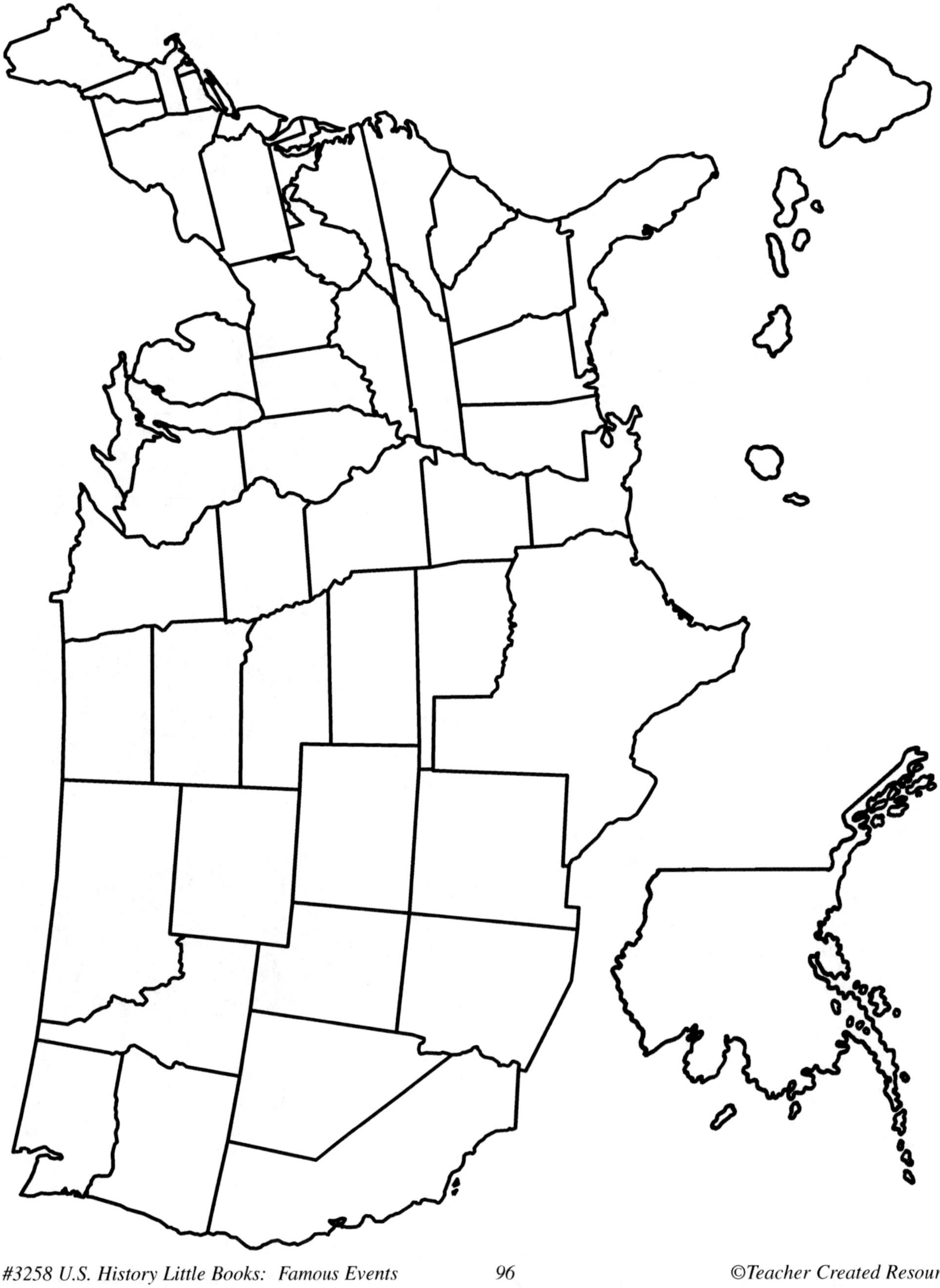

When did your state become part of the United States? ______________

Putting Together
The Growth of the U.S.A.

Materials

For each student you will need:

- copies of each pattern
- a stapler
- markers
- scissors (optional)

Note: Determine ahead of time if students' cutting skills will enable them to cut out the interiors of the maps. If not, arrange to have the cutting done ahead of time. Parents/helpers may choose to use craft knives instead of scissors.

Option: If cutting will be too difficult for students, make one large class book and laminate the pages.

Assembly Directions for the Layered Book

1. Cut out the pages of the book.

2. Seven of the pages have black areas which should be carefully cut out.

3. Page 8 of the layered book is of the continental United States. Use markers to outline the different sections of the United States. Make sure that each section is a different color.

   Option: Add the dates that each section became part of the United States.

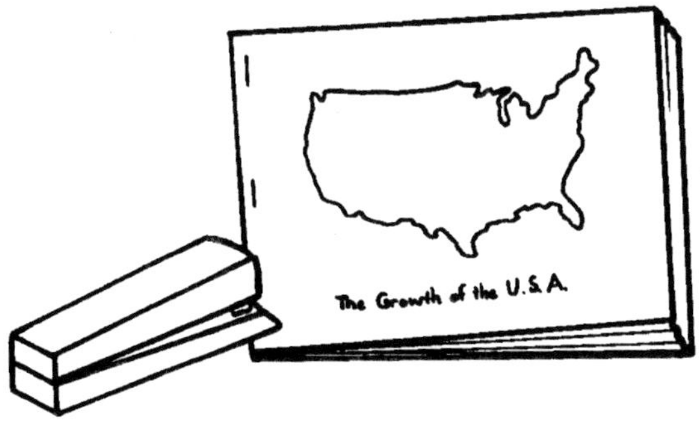

4. Layer the book in numerical order with the cover on top. There are nine pages altogether.

5. Staple down the left-hand side of the stacked pages.

The Growth of the U.S.A.

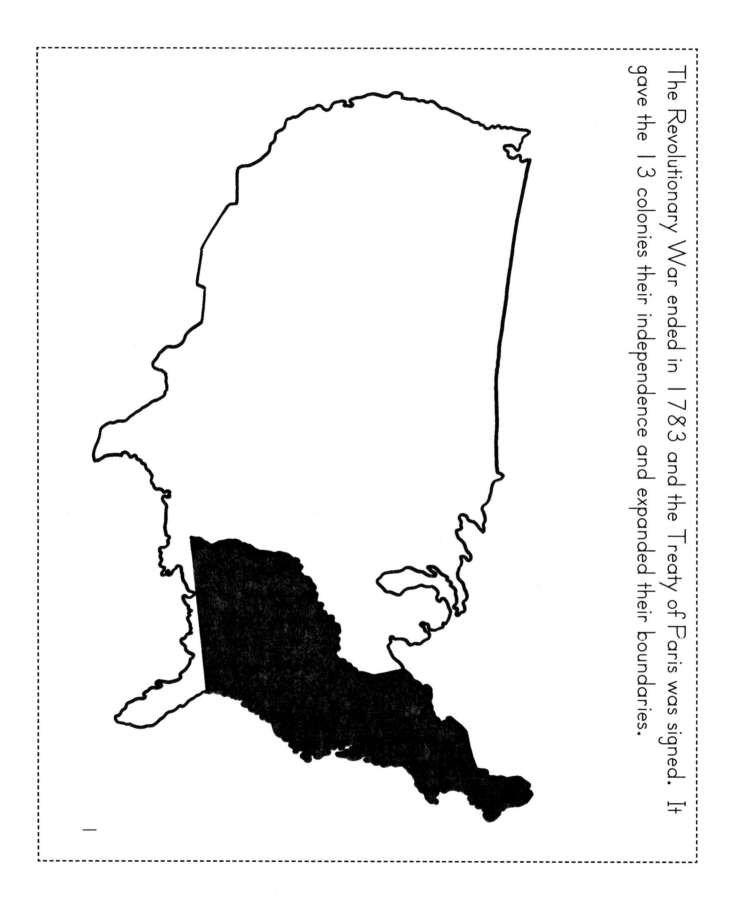

The Revolutionary War ended in 1783 and the Treaty of Paris was signed. It gave the 13 colonies their independence and expanded their boundaries.

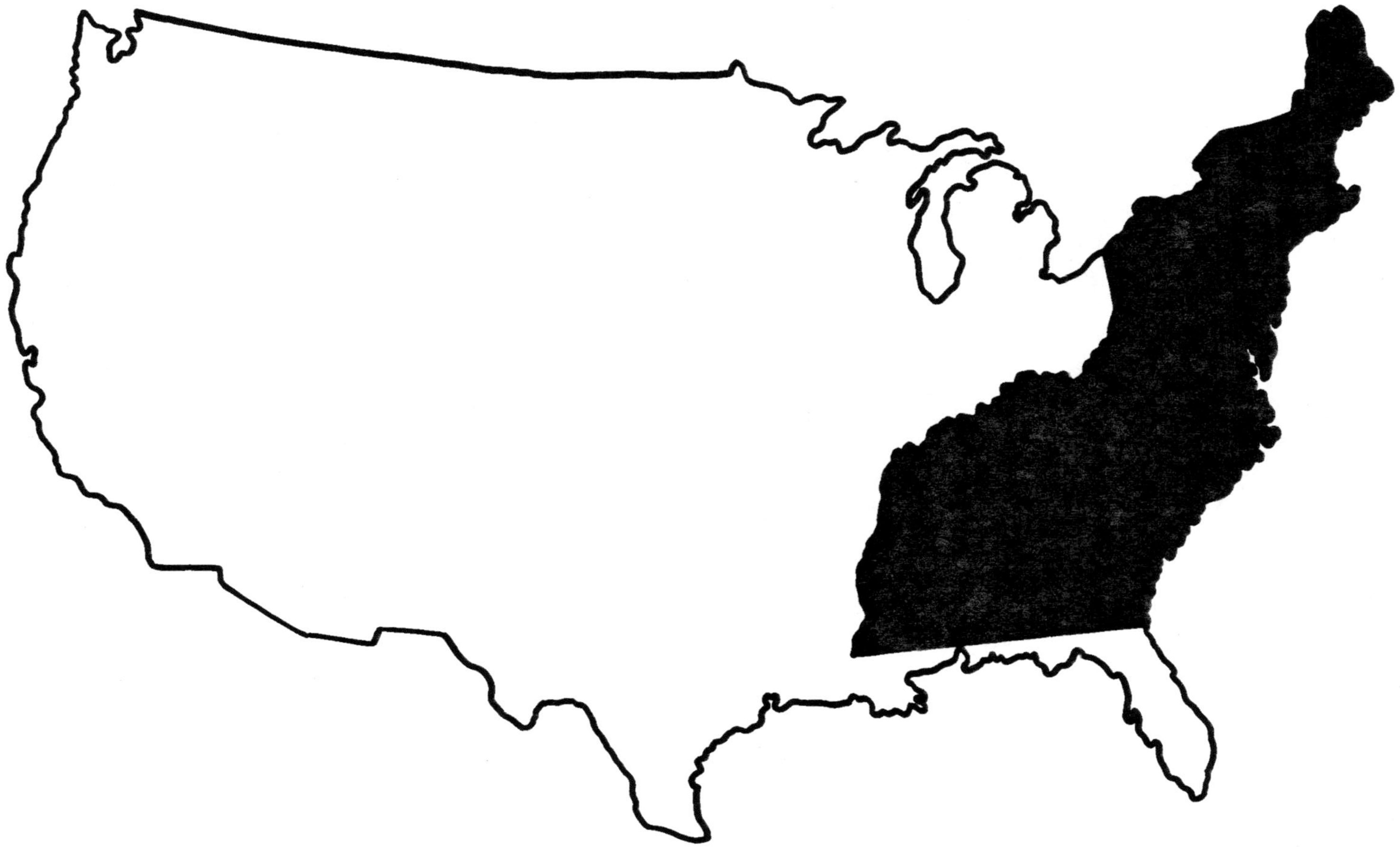

1

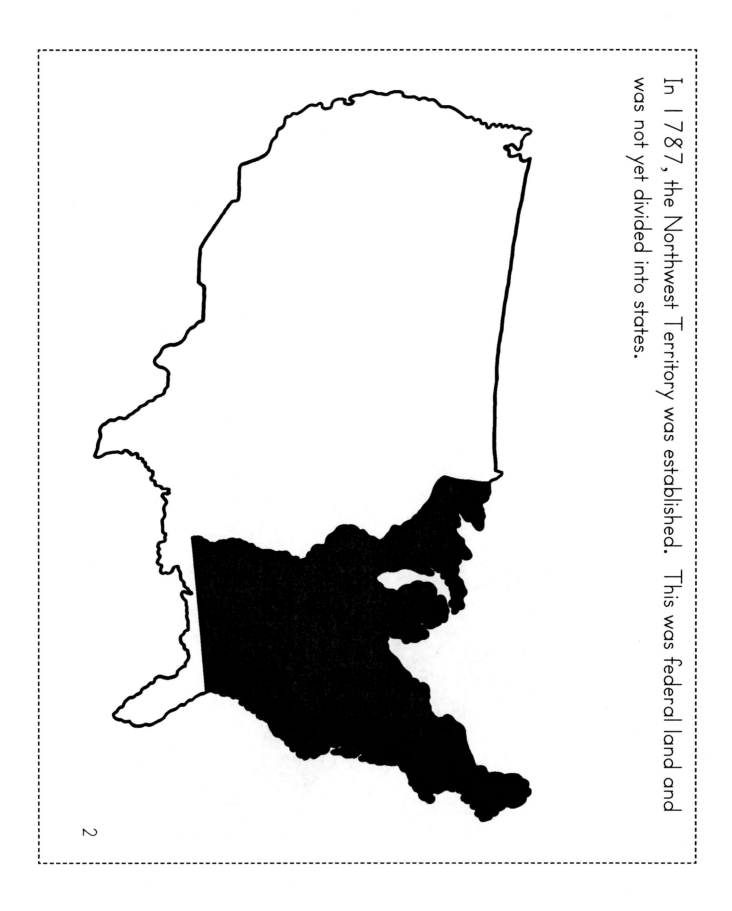

In 1787, the Northwest Territory was established. This was federal land and was not yet divided into states.

2

The Louisiana Purchase was made in 1803. The land that doubled the size of the United States was bought from France for 15 million dollars.

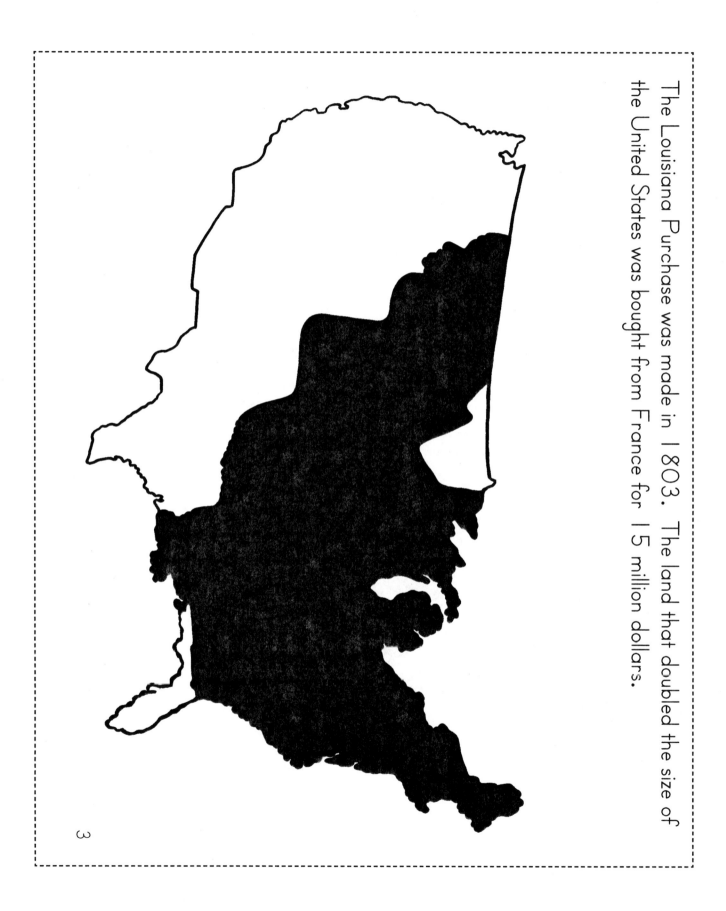

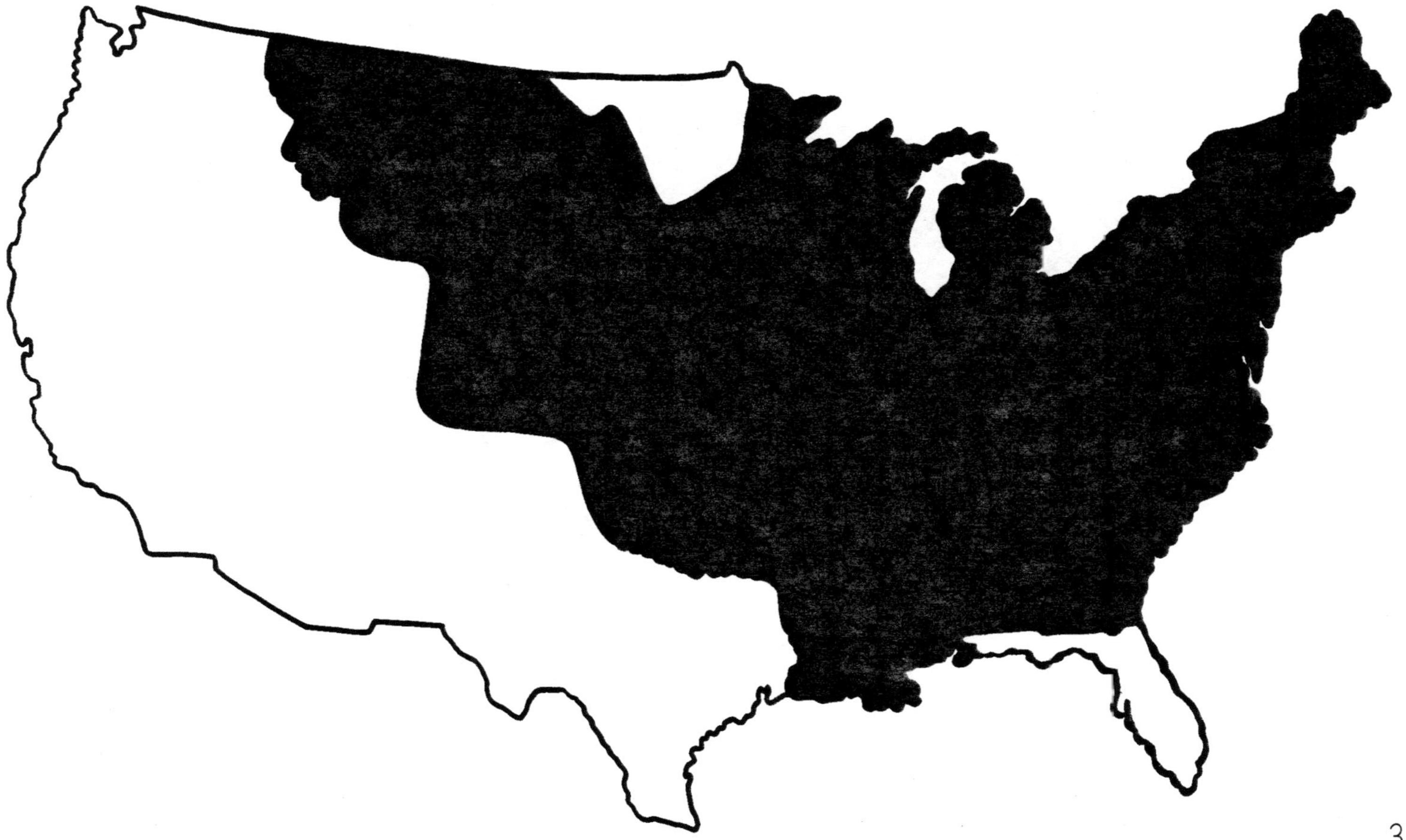

3

In 1818, Great Britain gave the United States some land to the west of the Northwest Territory (Red River cession). The same year the United States won Florida from Spain.

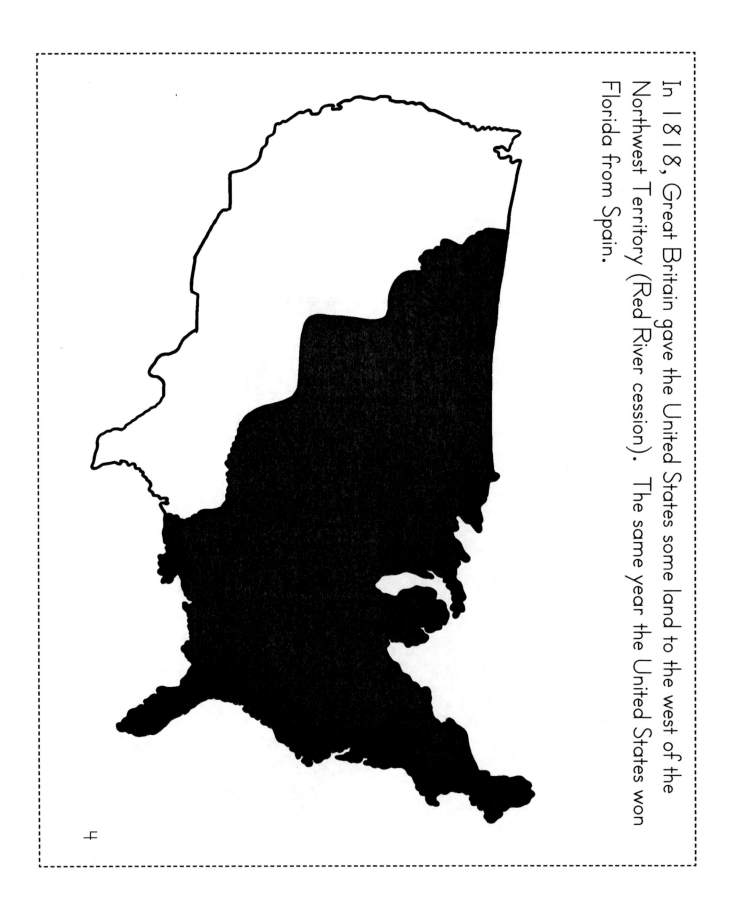

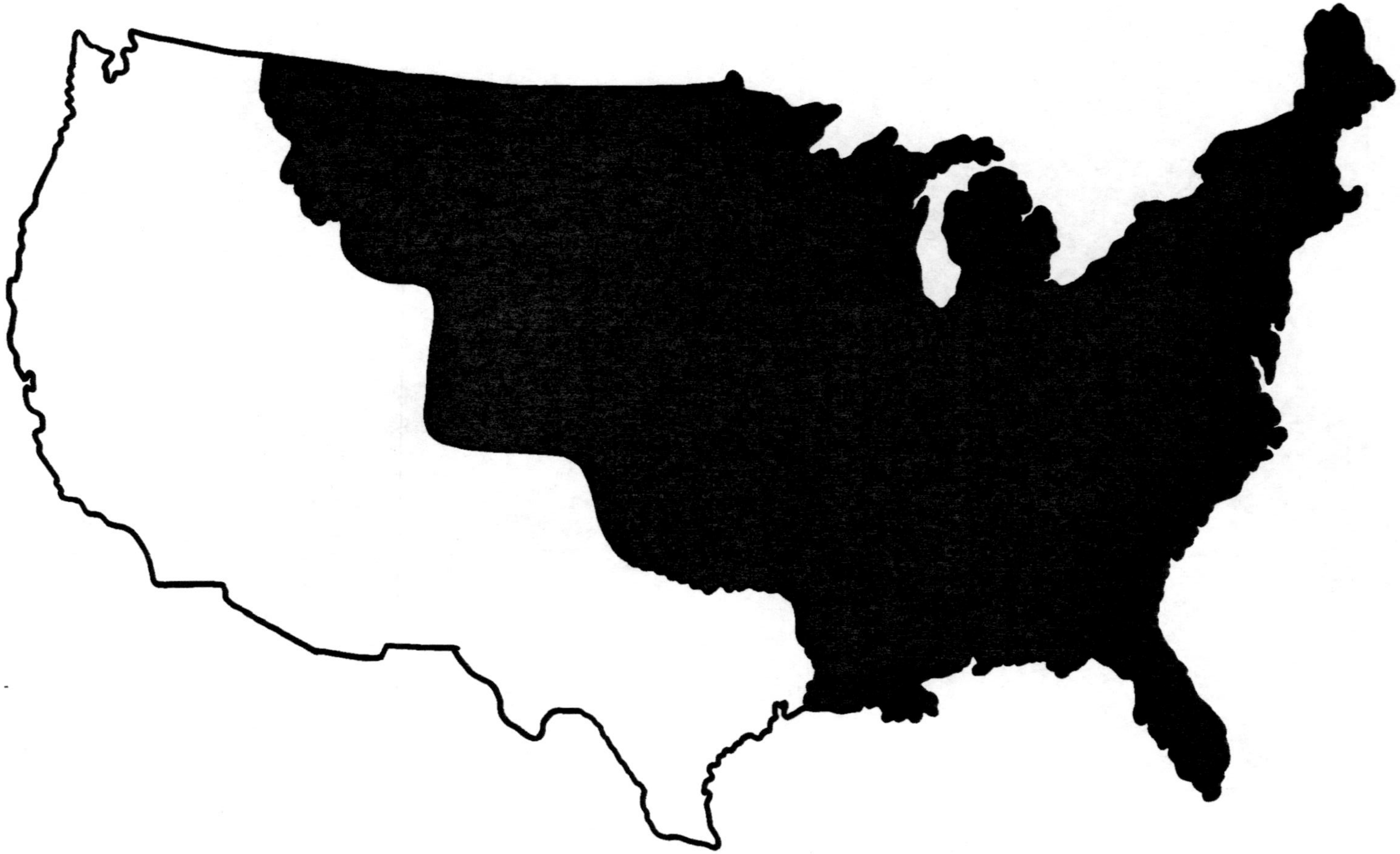

4

Texas was annexed from Mexico in 1845.

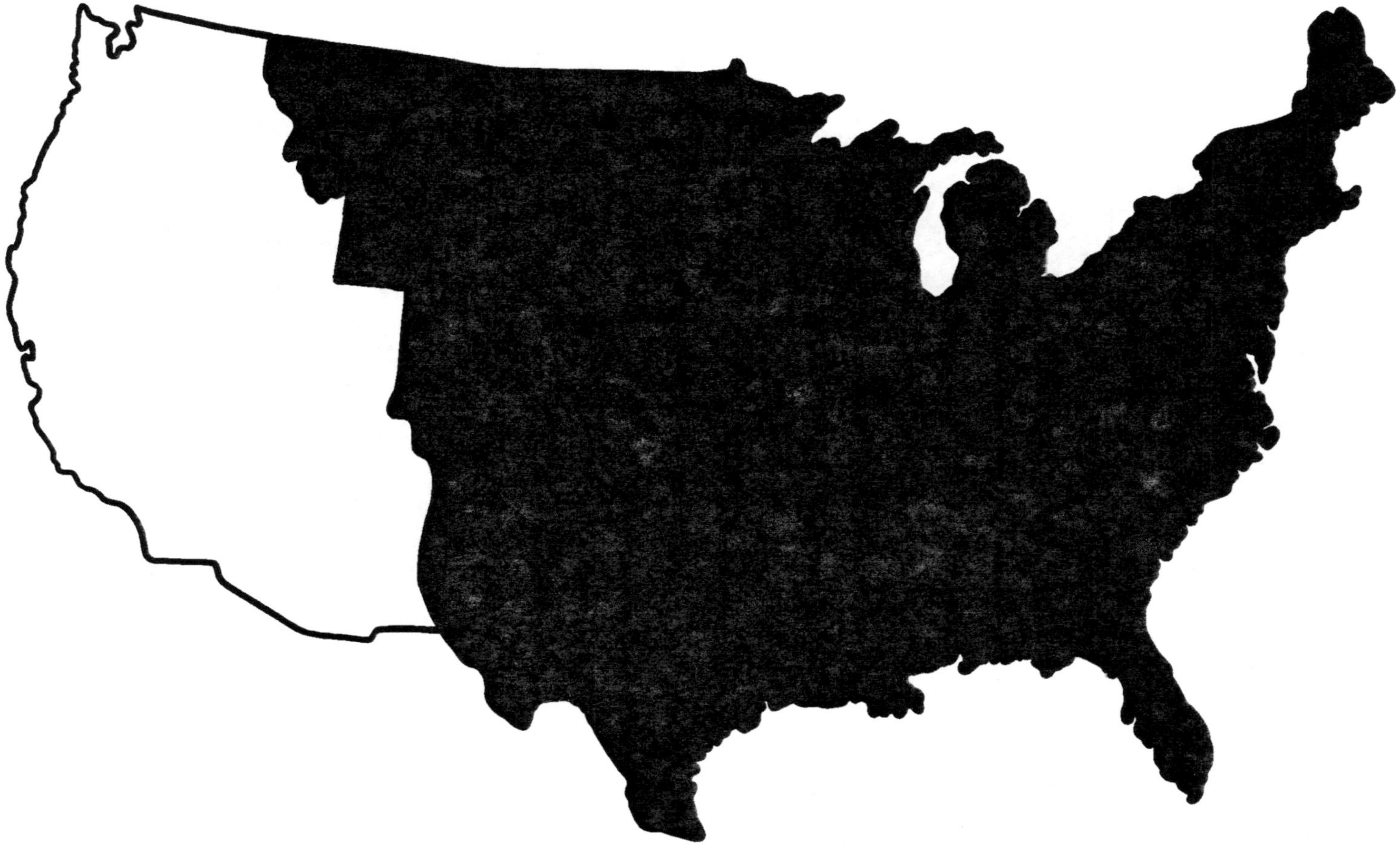

5

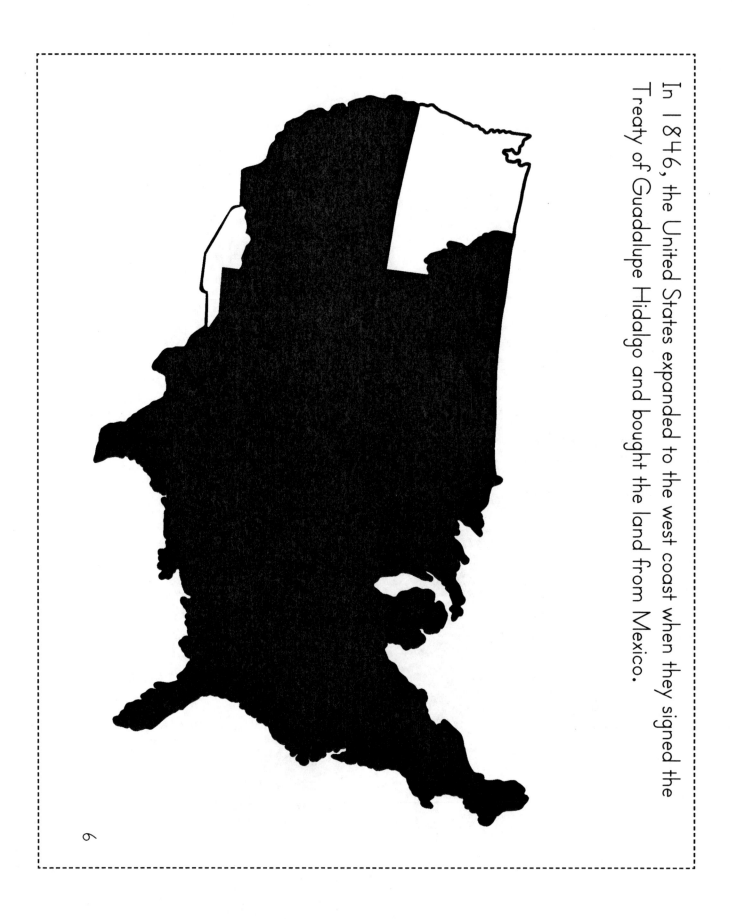

In 1846, the United States expanded to the west coast when they signed the Treaty of Guadalupe Hidalgo and bought the land from Mexico.

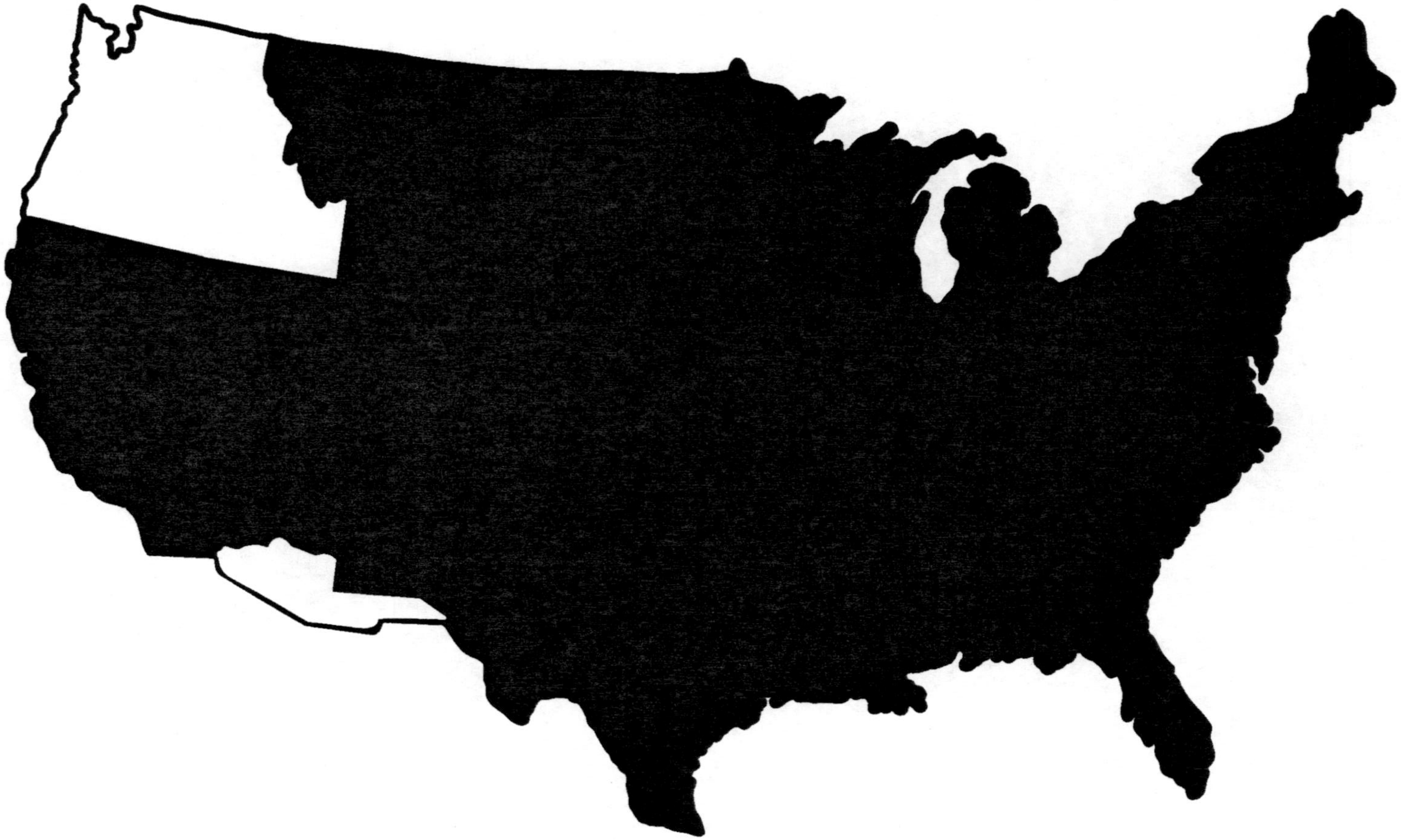

6

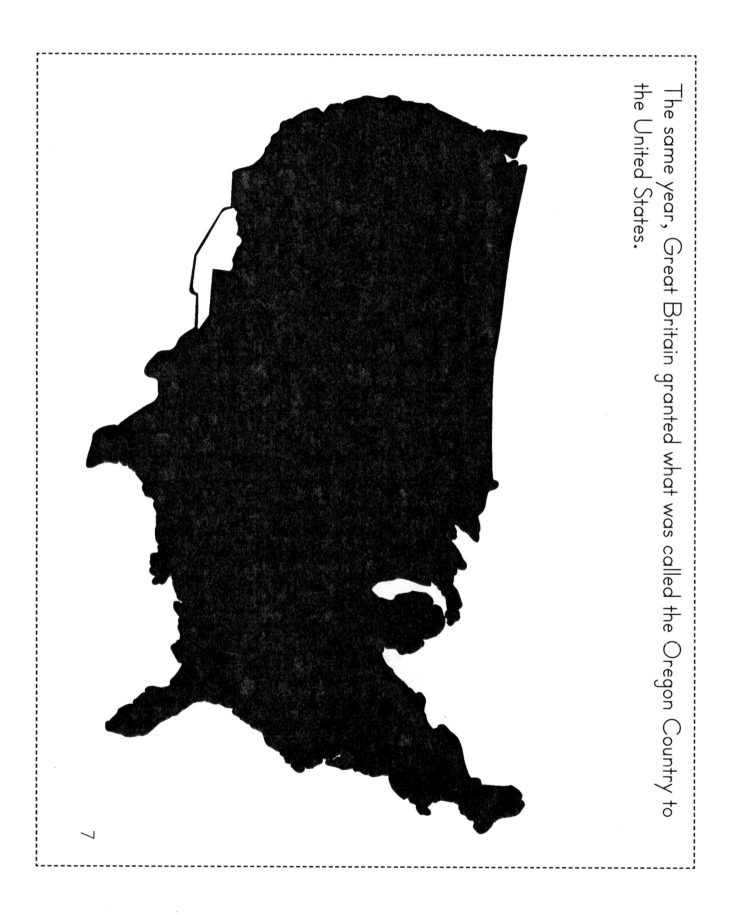

The same year, Great Britain granted what was called the Oregon Country to the United States.

7

In 1853, more land was acquired from Mexico in the Gadsden Purchase.

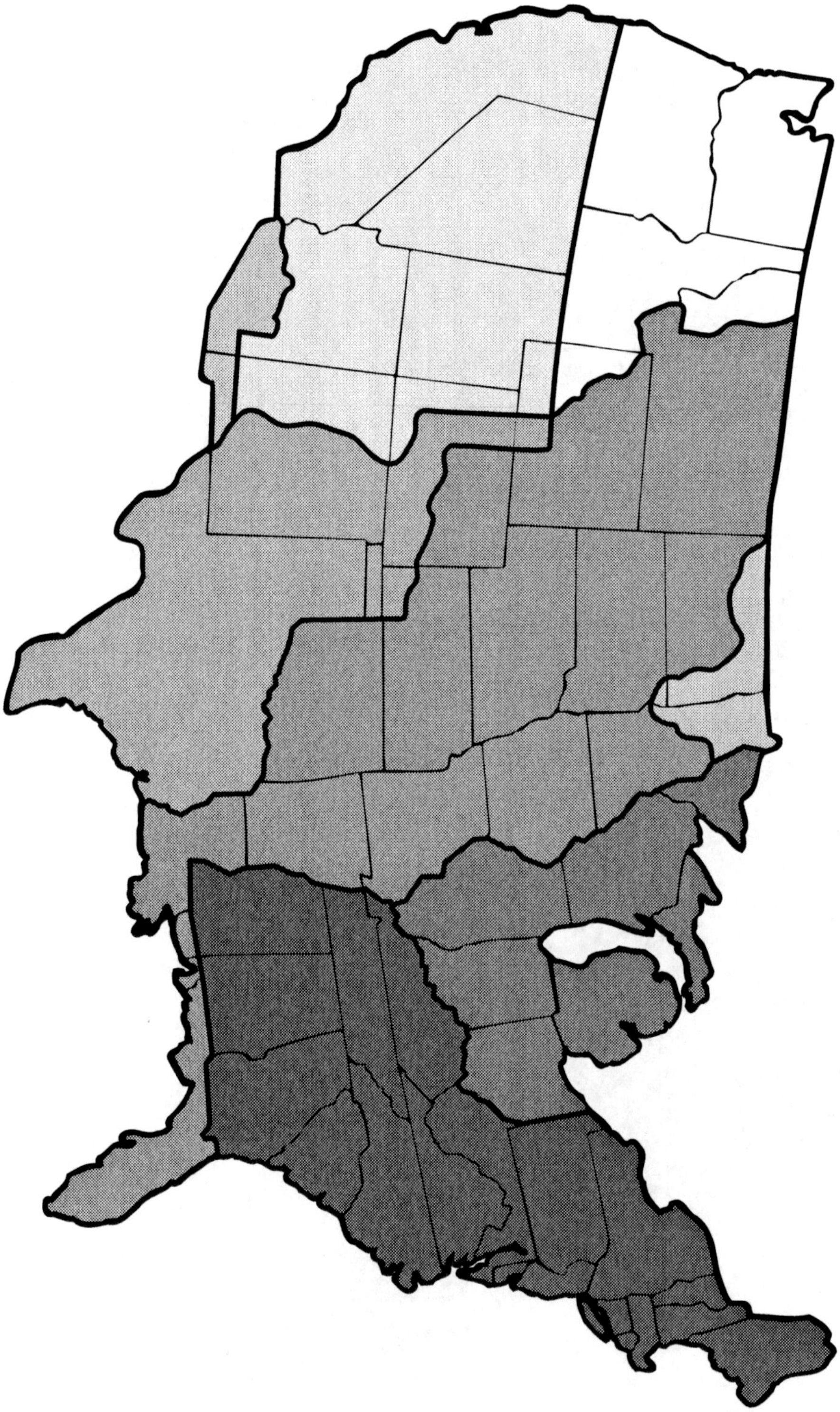

8

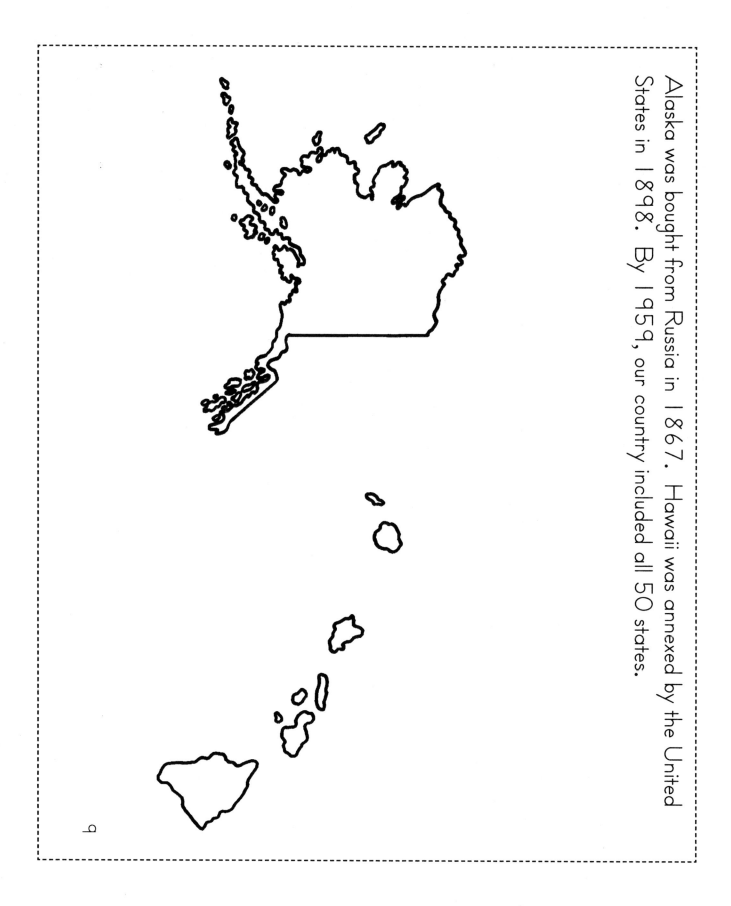

Alaska was bought from Russia in 1867. Hawaii was annexed by the United States in 1898. By 1959, our country included all 50 states.

©Teacher Created Resources, Inc.

The National Anthem

Frances Scott Key was an attorney in Georgetown at the time of the War of 1812. The war was fought because Britain was trying to regulate shipping in America. The British had raided Washington, D.C., which was located very near to Georgetown. The Americans were preparing for an attack on Baltimore next. The commander of Fort McHenry in Baltimore had asked for a huge flag so that "the British would have no trouble seeing it from a distance."

Word spread that the British had captured an elderly man named Dr. William Beanes. Frances Scott Key was asked to try to rescue him. He agreed to go and was accompanied by an agent for prisoner exchange named Col. John Skinner. They went on board the flagship, *Tonnant*, where Dr. Beanes was being held. The British would not consider releasing Dr. Beanes. When the men produced letters from British prisoners speaking of how well they had been treated under Dr. Beanes' care, the British changed their minds. They finally said that the doctor could go but that they would not be released until after the attack on Fort McHenry because they knew too much of what the British were planning.

Frances Scott Key waited through hours of battle with bombs lighting up the sky. On September 14, 1814, Mr. Key waited in the dark knowing that at the first sign of light, he would be able to see if the flag was still waving. If the flag at the fort was still waving, it would mean that America had won the battle. When he saw the flag, he was so excited that he began to write a poem about the experience. He was released, and the next night he finished writing the poem in the Indian Queen Hotel in Baltimore.

Key's brother-in-law, Judge J.H. Nicholson, had the poem printed and it was called "Defense of Fort McHenry." As the poem began circulating in America, it began to gain popularity. It was put to the tune of a song called "Anacreon in Heaven." An actor sang it in October at a function and called it "The Star-Spangled Banner."

The song was used as a patriotic song through the years and in 1916, President Woodrow Wilson recognized it as the national anthem, but it was still not enacted into law. In 1931, a polling group asked a magazine called *Current Events* if they would ask schoolchildren all over the United States to vote on whether the song should be our national anthem. The polling group did not like the song. They thought it was too hard to sing and the words were too militant. The schoolchildren had three choices to pick from: "America the Beautiful," "The Star Spangled Banner," and "America." The students picked "The Star Spangled Banner" by a majority of 2 to 1. After these results became public, it became a law that was signed in 1931 by President Herbert Hoover.

The Star-Spangled Banner

by Francis Scott Key

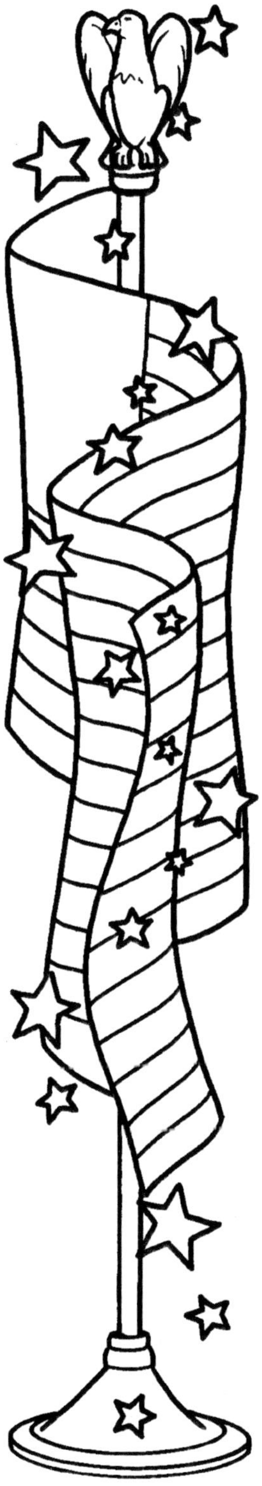

Oh! say, can you see, by the dawn's early light,
What so proudly we hailed at the twilight's last gleaming?
Whose broad stripes and bright stars, through the perilous fight,
O'er the ramparts we watched were so gallantly streaming?
And the rockets' red glare, the bombs bursting in air,
Gave proof through the night that our flag was still there.
Oh! say, does that star-spangled banner yet wave
O'er the land of the free and the home of the brave?

On the shore, dimly seen through the midst of the deep,
Where the foe's haughty host in dread silence reposes,
What is that which the breeze, o'er the towering steep,
As it fitfully blows, half conceals, half discloses?
Now it catches the gleam of the morning's first beam,
In full glory reflected, now shines on the stream.
"Tis the star-spangled banner. Oh! long may it wave
O'er the land of the free and the home of the brave!

Oh! thus be it ever, when free men shall stand
Between their loved homes and the war's desolation!
Blest with vict'ry and peace, may the Heav'n-rescued land
Praise the Pow'r that hath made and preserved us a nation.
Then conquer we must, when our cause it is just,
And this be our motto, "In God is our trust."
And the star-spangled banner in triumph shall wave
O'er the land of the free and the home of the brave.

The National Anthem

Map Study

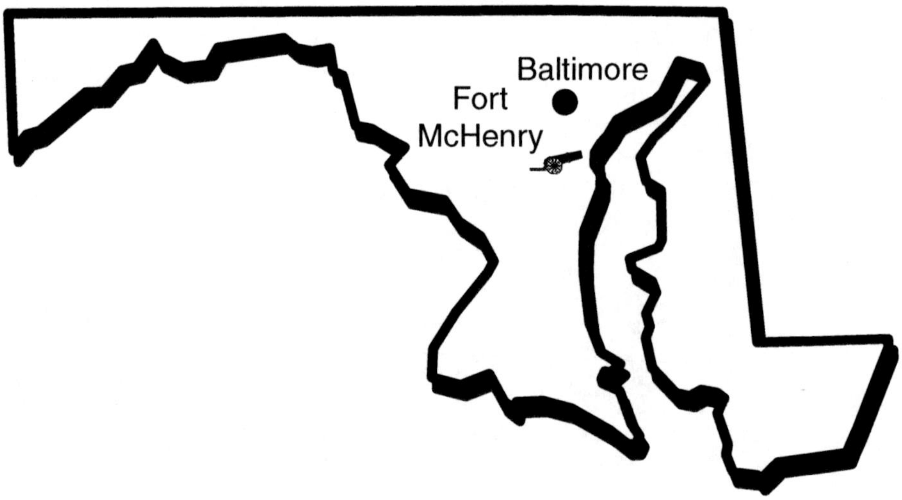

Frances Scott Key wrote part of *The Star-Spangled Banner* during the British attack of Fort McHenry near Baltimore, Maryland.

Putting Together
The National Anthem

Materials

For each student you will need:

- one copy of the text page (page 112)
- one copy of each of the illustration pages (pages 113–114)
- one copy of "The Star Spangled Banner" (page 109)
- 4 sheets of white copy paper
- one 9" x 12" sheet of red construction paper
- one 4½" x 5" piece of blue construction paper or the star template (page 115)
- 50 stars–Use star stickers or punch outs from a star hole punch (optional)

Preparation for the *National Anthem* Layered Book

1. Cut the four white sheets of copy paper. The pages should measure as follows: 4½" x 11", 5¾" x 11", and 7" x 11". Trim the last page ¼" from the top to measure 8¼" x 11".
2. Trim the red paper to 9" x 11". To create the red stripes for the flag, cut the trimmed sheet into seven strips, each measuring ⅝" x 11".
3. Color the song page.

Assembly Directions for the *National Anthem* Layered Book

Top Page

1. Glue a red stripe at the top of the 4½" x 11" sheet; glue a second stripe at the bottom of the sheet. Evenly space two more stripes in between them.
2. Cut a 4½" x 5" piece of blue construction paper and glue it to the left side. Glue 50 stars in rows to the blue construction paper. The top row should have six stars and the second row will have five stars. Alternate rows of six stars and five stars until all 50 stars have been applied. Option: Instead of using blue construction paper and stars, color and glue the star pattern provided (page 115.)

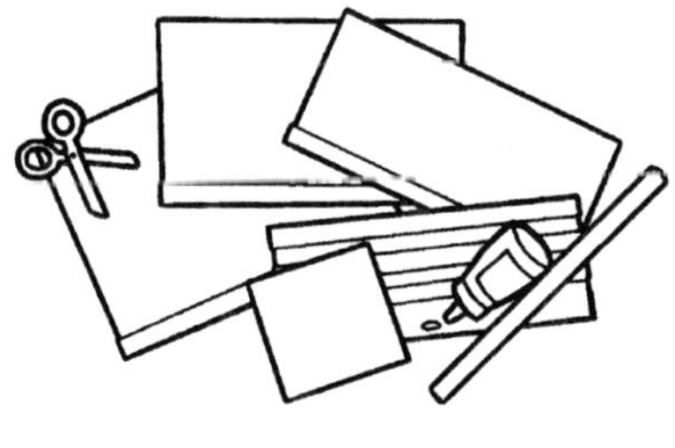

Pages 2–4

1. Glue one red stripe to the bottom of each page.
2. Layer the book with the largest page on the bottom and the smallest page on top.
3. Make sure that the tops and left sides of the pages are lined up evenly. Red and white stripes should be visible all the way down the flag. Double-check that there are 13 stripes.
4. Staple down the left side of the flag. Make certain that the blue section is the top left section.
5. Attach the text and the illustrations to the appropriate pages.
6. Glue a copy of the song to the back page of the book.

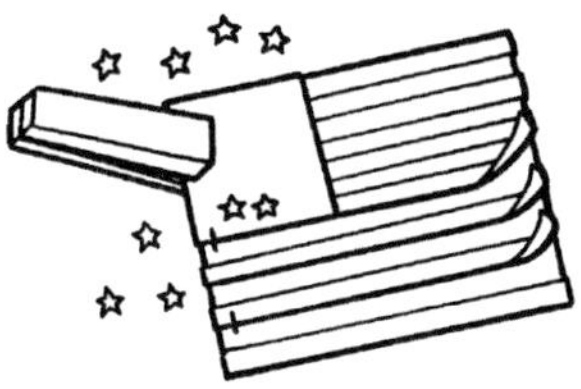

The National Anthem

Layered Book Text

During the War of 1812, the British had captured a prisoner named Dr. William Beanes. An attorney named Frances Scott Key was asked to try to rescue him. 1

The British said they would not release Dr. Beanes, Mr. Key, or his companion until after they attacked Fort McHenry. 2

Frances Scott Key watched from a ship in the early morning hours after the attack to see if the flag was still flying at the fort. When he saw the flag, he knew that America had won the battle. It inspired him to write what we know today as "The Star-Spangled Banner." 3

 ©Teacher Created Resources, Inc.

The National Anthem

Illustrations for Layered Book

Page 1

Page 2

The National Anthem

Illustrations for Layered Book

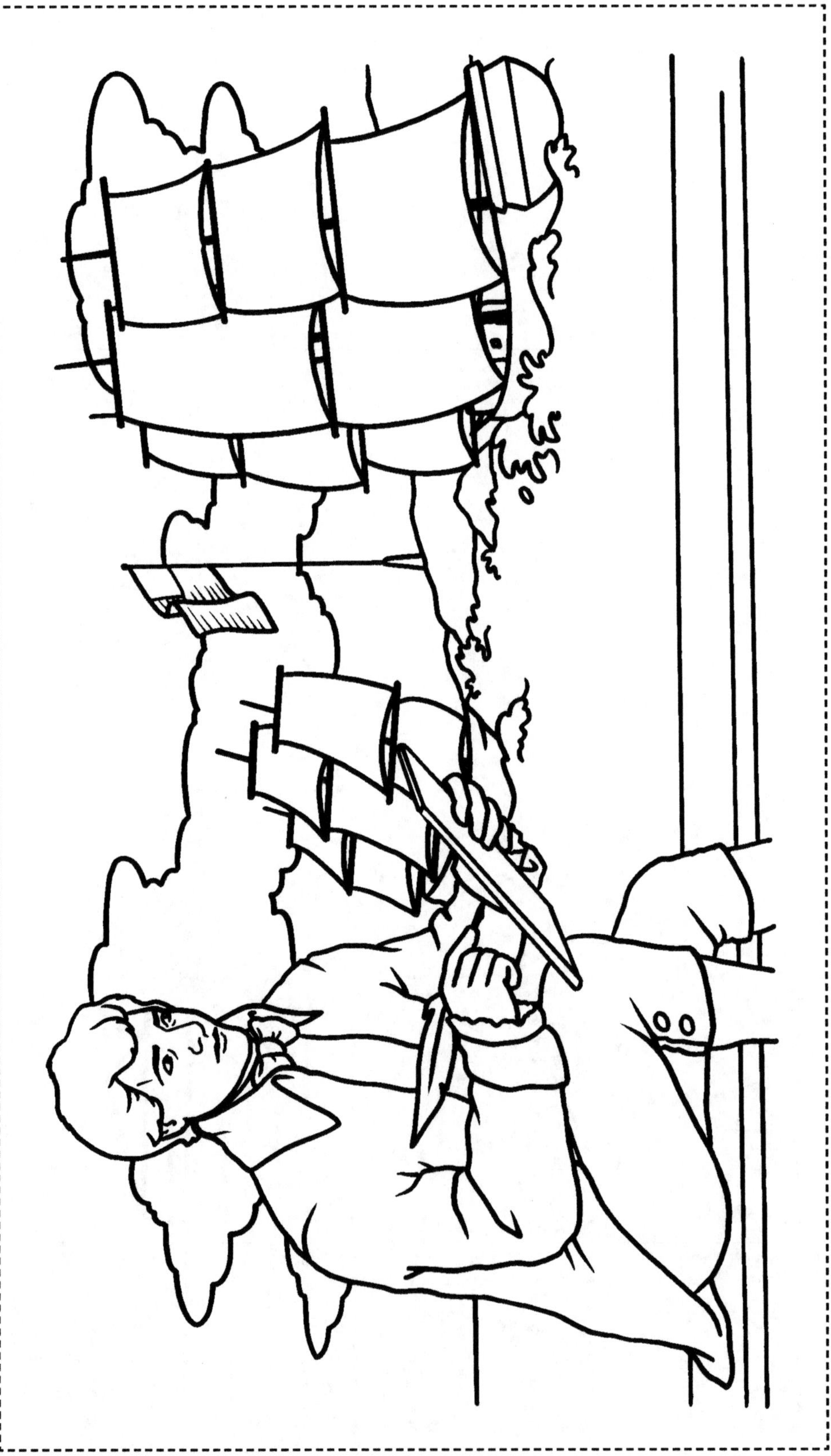

Page 3

The National Anthem

Template for Layered Book Cover

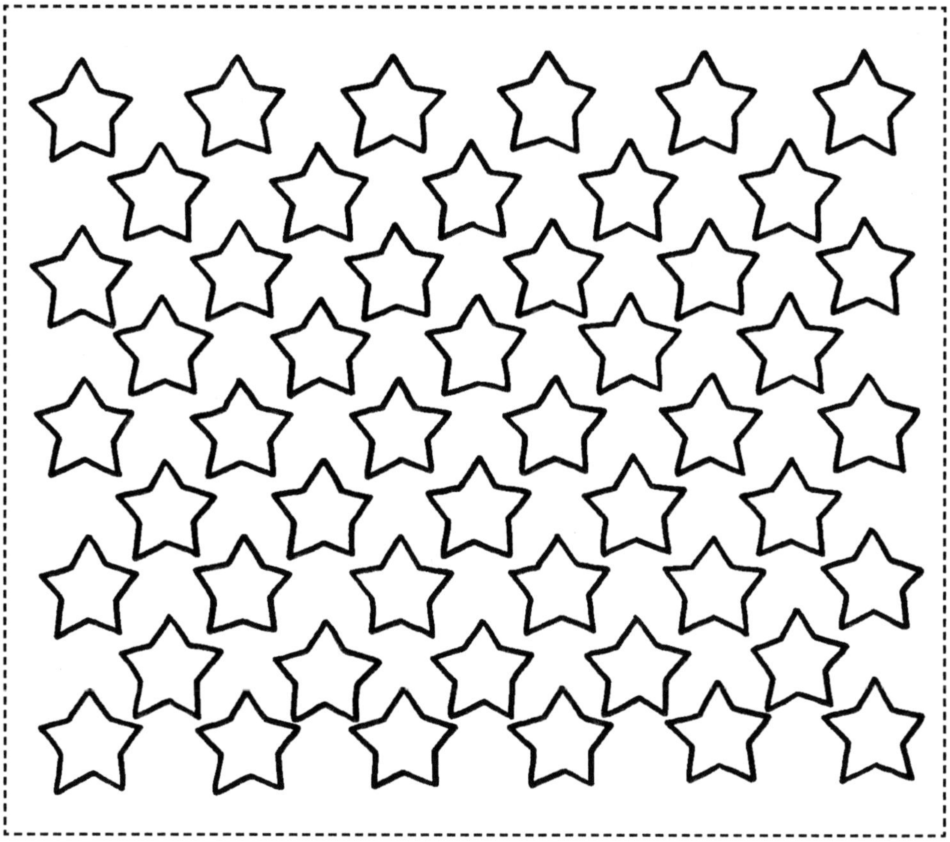

The First Thanksgiving

English Pilgrims suffered a long first winter in the New World. They were involved in their spring planting when they were approached by a friendly native. He identified himself in English as Samoset, representative of the Wampanoag community. A week later, two more natives came to meet with the Pilgrims. They were Squanto, who also spoke English, and his chief, Massasoit. Together with the settlers' governor, John Carver, the three men wrote a treaty by which both peoples would agree to live peacefully together. The laws of this treaty were honored for the next 50 years.

Squanto was a welcome friend to the Pilgrims. He shared his great knowledge of the land with them. He taught them the habits of the animals. Squanto also showed the Pilgrims how to trap lobster, to hunt deer, and to fish. He also showed them how to plant corn and beans, and which nuts and berries could be eaten. The end result was a bountiful harvest for the Pilgrims. Growing food indigenous to the area proved to be very important to their survival.

The Pilgrims had a celebration to acknowledge this great harvest of 1621. They invited Squanto, Chief Massasoit, and a few friends. In the middle of the street, tables were set up consisting of barrels with boards across them. The tables were topped with fine linen cloths. Much to the Pilgrims' surprise, over 90 natives appeared for the feast. Both Pilgrims and natives hunted for more fish and game. The women busied themselves preparing more vegetables and baked goods. Deer, turkey, seafood, bread, corn, pumpkins, peas, cranberries, and many other vegetables and fruits were served. The natives and Pilgrims ate their fill and entertained each other. The joyous celebration lasted for three days.

This first celebration of Thanksgiving occurred sometime in October. It was President Abraham Lincoln, in 1863, who deemed the last Thursday in November to be a national holiday of "thanksgiving and praise." Americans have honored this important event ever since. Many continue the tradition of preparing a large, festive meal and inviting friends, family, and loved ones to join them.

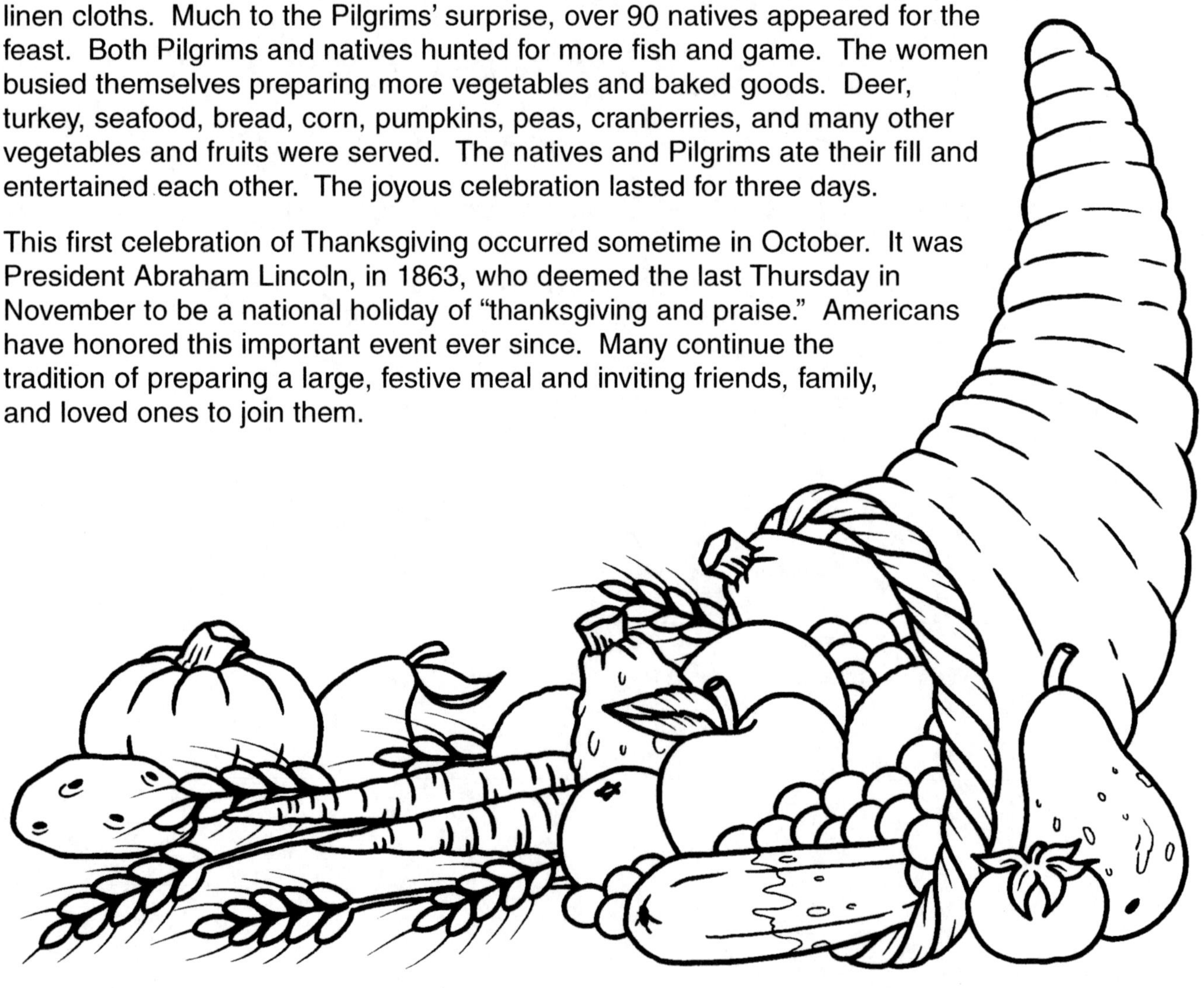

 ©Teacher Created Resources, Inc.

The First Thanksgiving

Map Study

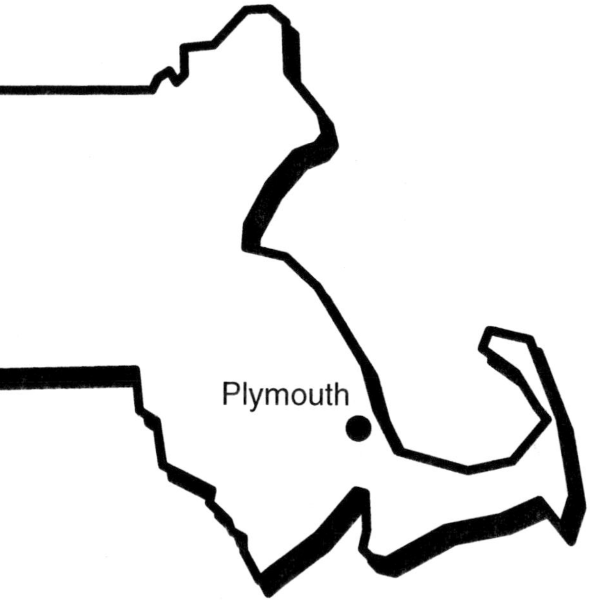

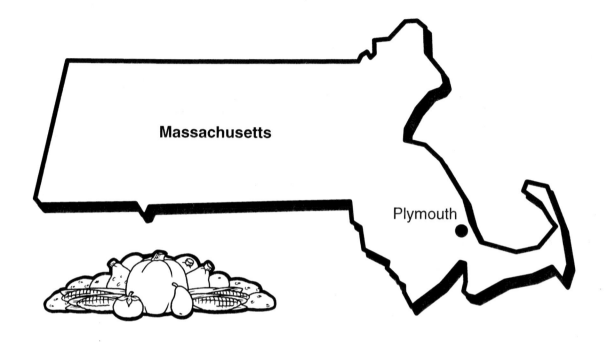

The first Thanksgiving took place in Plymouth, Massachusetts, in 1621.

Putting Together *The First Thanksgiving*

Materials

For each student you will need:

- copies of each sheet of text and flaps (pages 119–122)
- one sheet each of 9" x 12" green and light blue construction paper
- glue
- stapler
- markers or crayons
- scissors

Assembly Directions for the *First Thanksgiving* Lift-tab Book

1. To form the background, glue the blue and green construction paper together as shown, overlapping two inches.
2. Color the flaps. (**Note:** Remember that flaps are attached with a dot of glue to the top on the back of each flap.)
3. Cut out the text and the "picture flaps."
4. Glue or tape the tops (only) of the barrels to the green paper so that they sit along the bottom edge of the green paper.
5. Glue the top of the tablecloth just over the barrels so that the bottom half of the barrels are visible. Be sure to keep the area below the fold line of the tablecloth free of glue.
6. Glue the tops of the Pilgrim and the Native American next to each other so that they appear to be seated at the table.
7. Glue the tops of the fish and the vegetables to the left side of tabletop and glue the top of the turkey to the right side of tabletop.
8. Glue the text in the following order:

   text 1 under the Pilgrim
   text 2 under the Native American
   text 3 under the fish and vegetables
   text 4 under the turkey
   text 5 on underside of the vegetables
   text 6 and 7 under the barrels
9. Print the title, "The First Thanksgiving" on the top of the page.

The First Thanksgiving

Lift-tab Book Text

To celebrate the harvest of 1621, the Pilgrims of Plymouth had a feast. They invited Squanto, his chief, Massasoit, and a few friends. 1

Much to their surprise, over 90 natives came to the feast. They brought foods common to the area. 2

More fish, game, and other food was prepared. 3

Deer, turkey, seafood, bread, and many vegetables were served. 4

The natives and Pilgrims ate their fill, played games, and entertained each other. 5

The celebration lasted for three days. 6

President Abraham Lincoln declared the last Thursday in November to be a holiday of "thanks-giving and praise." 7

The First Thanksgiving

Illustrations

Table linen

 ©Teacher Created Resources, Inc.

The First Thanksgiving

Illustrations

Native American

Pilgrim

Turkey and fish

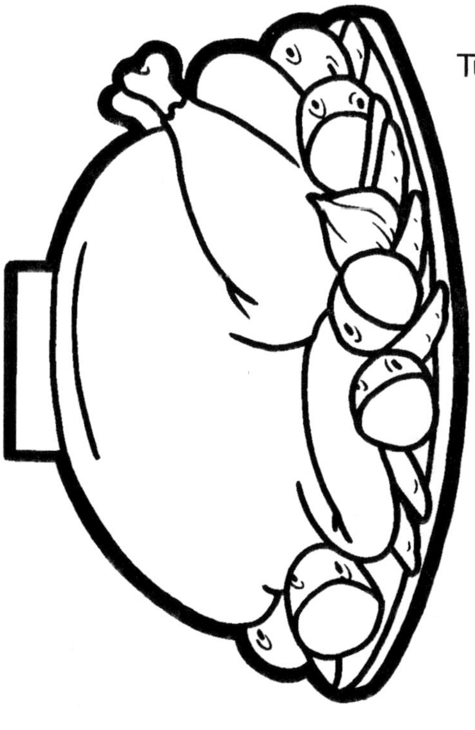

The First Thanksgiving

Illustrations

Vegetables

Barrel

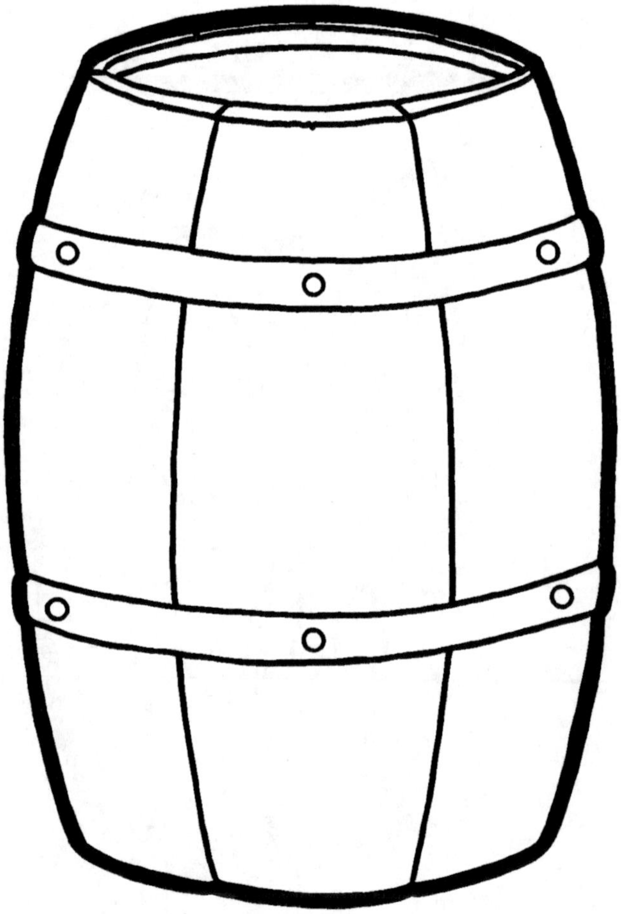

Barrel

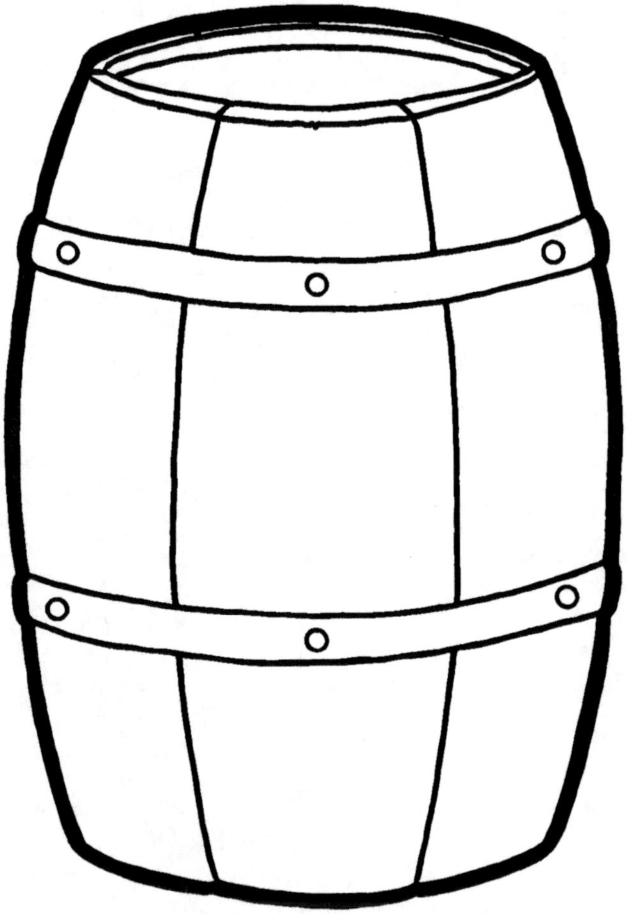

 ©Teacher Created Resources, Inc.

The Boston Tea Party

Everyone rejoiced at the end of the French and Indian War (1754–1763). The American colonists had helped the British win this seven-year conflict. The war had left Britain with a substantial debt so the British government taxed the American colonies. The Stamp Act created taxes on newspapers and legal documents. The colonists were furious and felt that they should not be taxed without representation in the British government. There was so much opposition by the colonists that the taxes were dropped on everything but tea. Tea, of course, was the colonists' favorite drink.

The most vocal group against the British rule was from Boston, Massachusetts. The leader among this group was Samuel Adams. Adams had graduated from Harvard. He was unsuccessful as a businessman, but excellent as a politician. He led the Committee of Correspondence, which was a group of letter writers formed to keep all of the neighboring areas abreast of major news. Adams also encouraged a secret club supporting independence. Paul Revere was a member of this club, called the Sons of Liberty. Other famous supporters of Samuel Adams were a wealthy merchant named John Hancock who later signed the Declaration of Independence and Samuel Adams' cousin, John Adams, an attorney, who later became the second president of the United States.

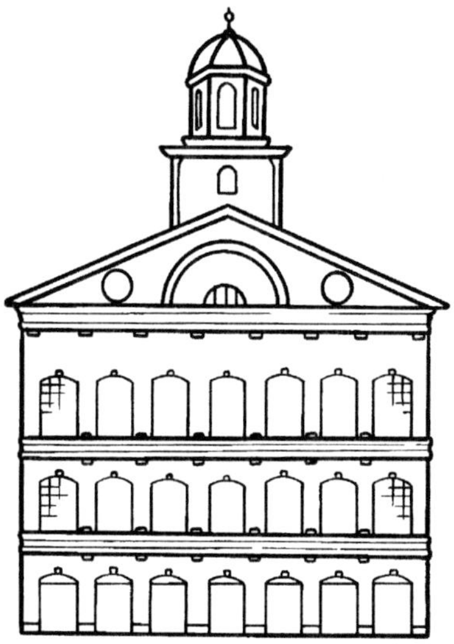

At first, the colonists avoided the tax on tea by not buying British tea. Instead, colonists bought smuggled Dutch tea. Later, the British would only allow The British East India Company to sell tea in the colonies. After this policy was enacted and the colonists saw the ships loaded with tea coming into the Boston Harbor, they sent Paul Revere on his horse to neighboring towns to tell others what was happening. The protesting colonists met in Faneuil Hall, the town meeting place, and decided not to unload the ships. In Philadelphia and New York, the protest worked and the ships went back to England with the tea. This strategy did not work in Boston. The Royal governor of Boston, Thomas Hutchinson, had connections with The British East India Company. His two sons worked for the tea company, and it would be devastating for them financially if the ships went back to England. The people went as a group to ask the tea company workers to meet with them and they refused. Governor Hutchinson finally gave the colonists an ultimatum. They would have until midnight on December 16, 1773, to pay the taxes on the tea or the tea would be removed from the ships by the army and stored. Neither the governor nor the tea company officials would relent.

On December 16, 1773, men dressed up like Mohawk Indians. They carried axes and went down to the docks. Each group of men boarded one of the three ships at Griffins Wharf. The Sons of Liberty ordered the crews of the ship to open the areas with the chests of tea. The 342 chests of tea were hauled up by the disguised men. They emptied all the chests into the Boston Harbor. This event was later named the Boston Tea Party. It infuriated the British Parliament and they closed Boston Harbor to all ships. Massachusetts was put under military rule. The Revolutionary War began 16 months later.

The Boston Tea Party

Map Study

The Boston Tea Party occurred in Boston Harbor on December 16, 1773.

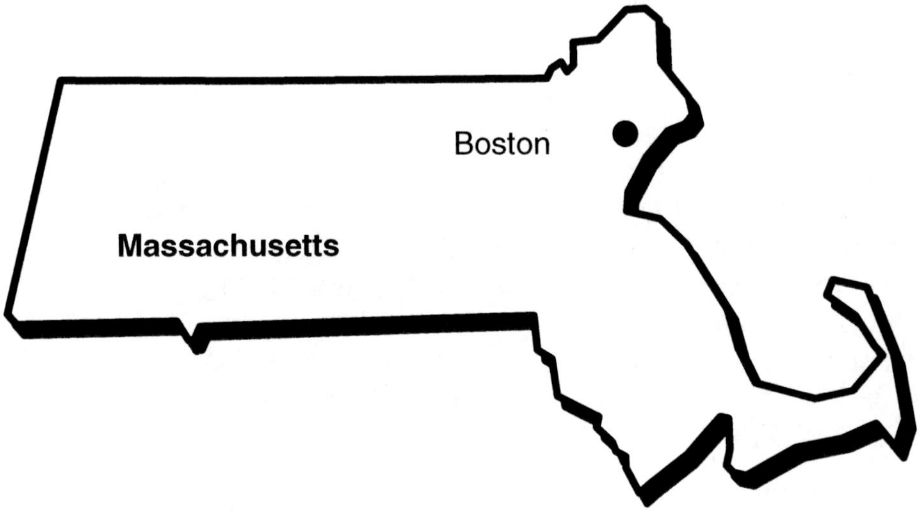

Can you label the
13 original colonies?

Putting Together
The Boston Tea Party

Materials for the Lift-tab Book

For each student you will need:

- copies of each of the pages
- copies of each of the lift-tabs
- $^1/_2$ teaspoon of dried tea leaves or contents of teabag
- a stapler
- crayons or markers
- scissors

Assembly Directions

1. Color each page. Trim the edges of the page along the dashed lines.
2. Cut a slit on page 4 where indicated (top of trunk).
3. Place the text strips in the appropriate crates.
4. Color the flaps (crate lids) and cut them out. Tape or glue them to the appropriate spaces on each tea crate.
5. Cut out the tea pull-tab for page 4. Fold the top and bottom tabs under.
6. Glue some loose tea to the front of the pull-tab and let it dry.
7. Insert the tea pull-tab. The pull-tab should come through the slit to the front side. The tea leaves should show.
8. Fold and stack the pages in numerical order.
9. Staple down the left side of the booklet.

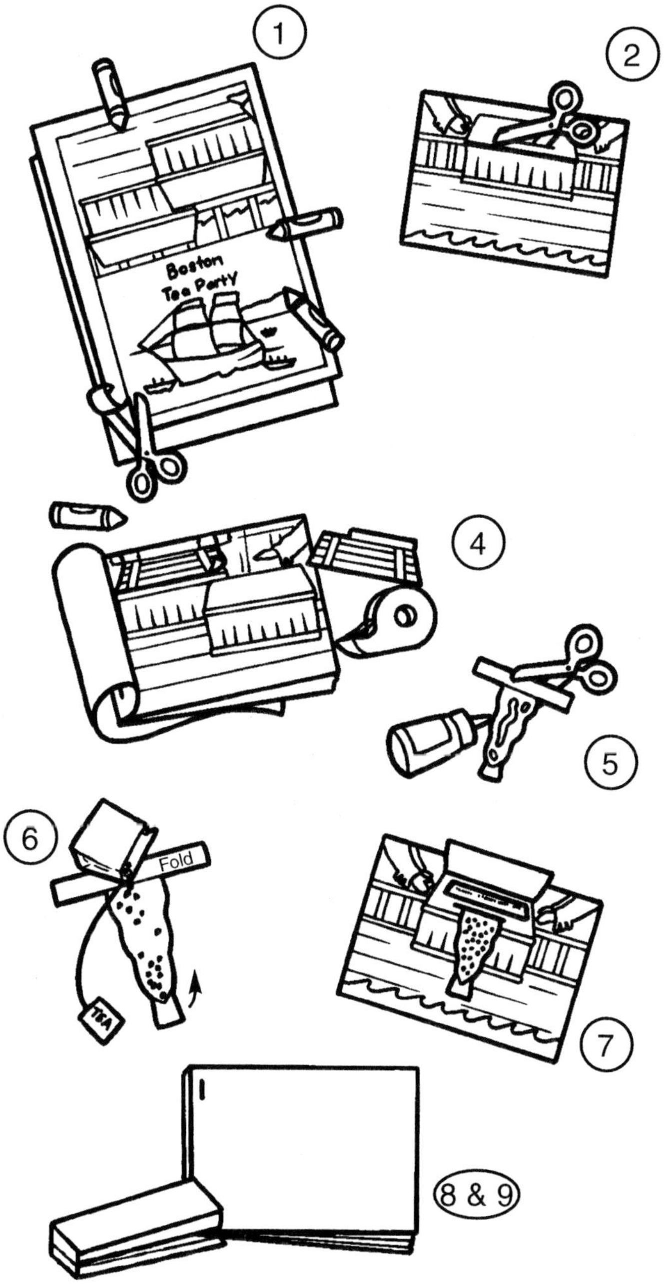

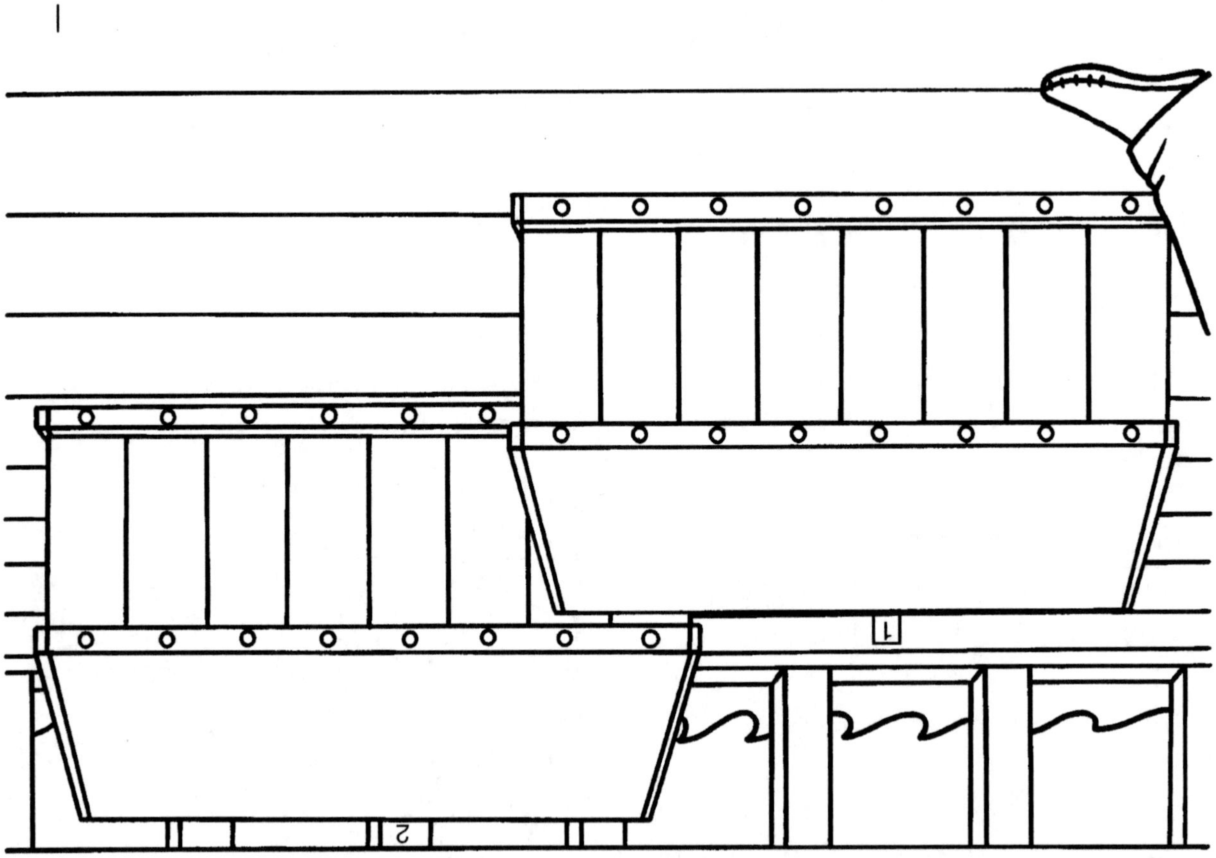

The Boston Tea Party

3

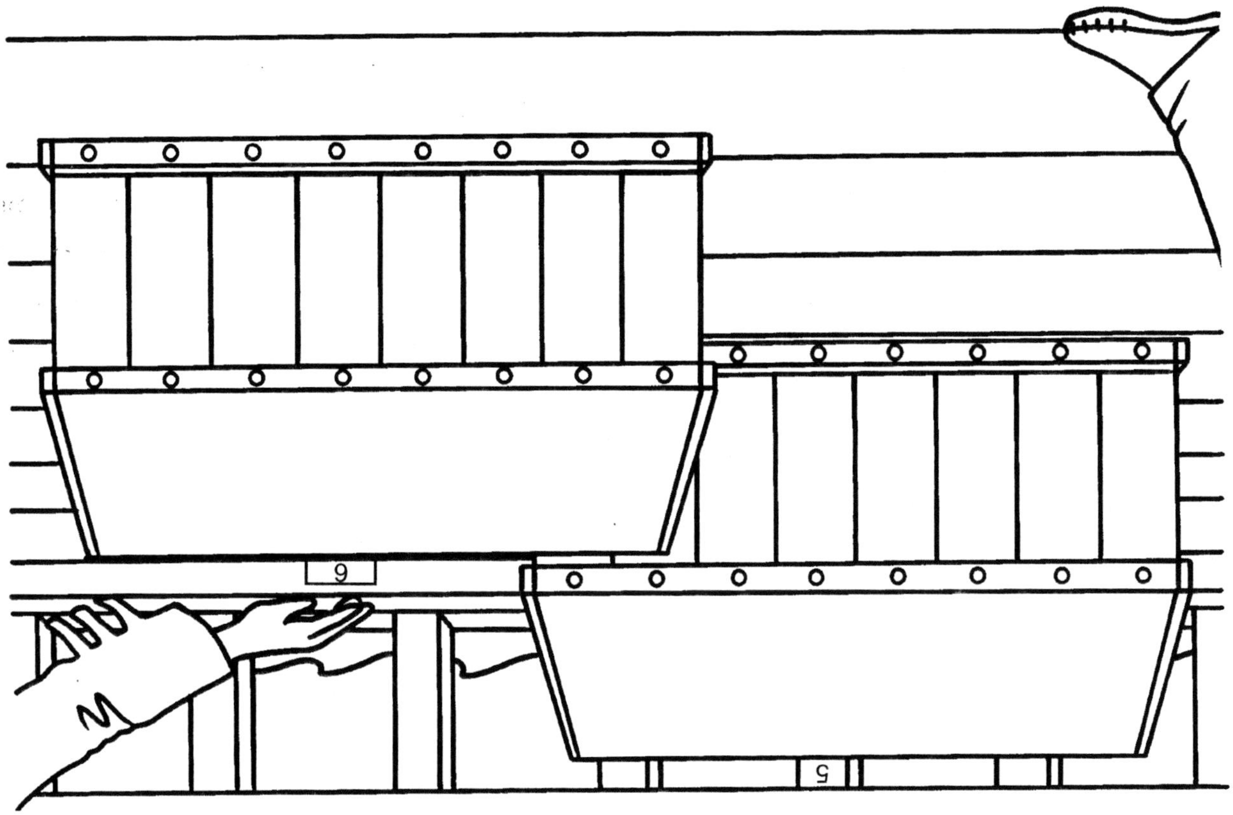

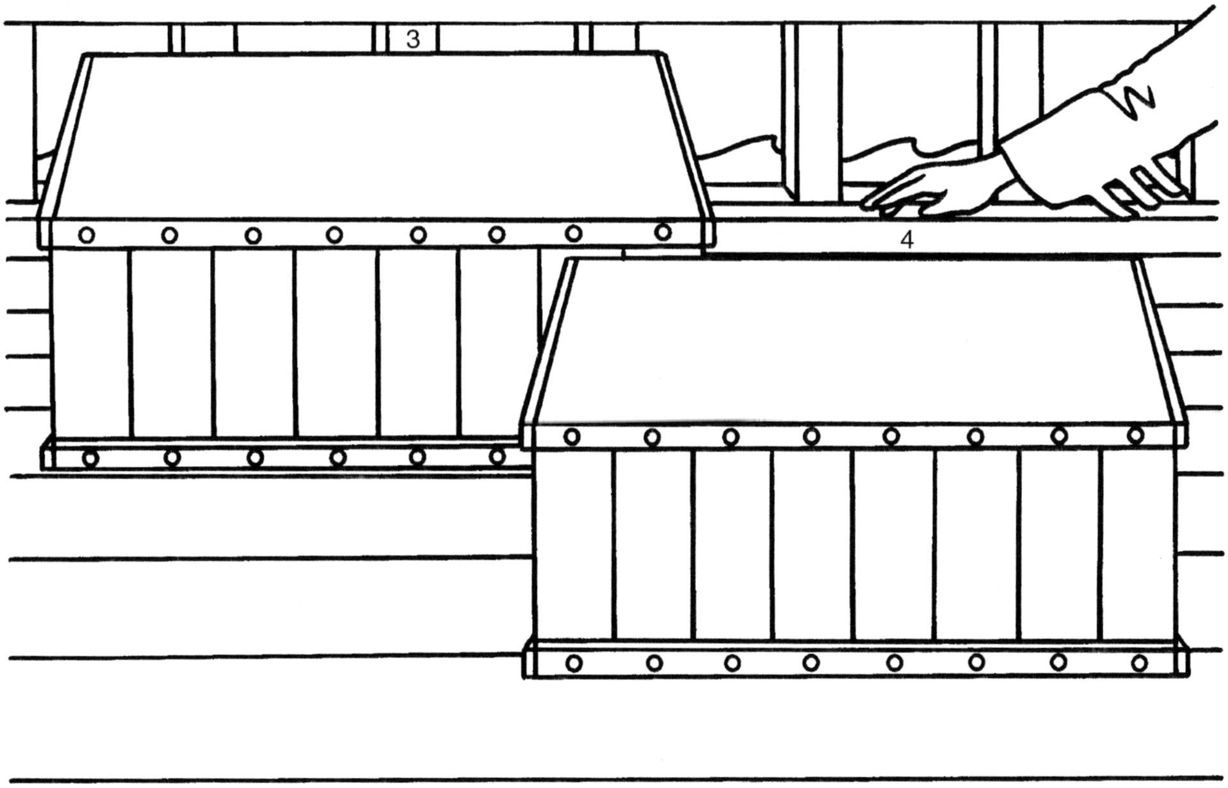

2

7

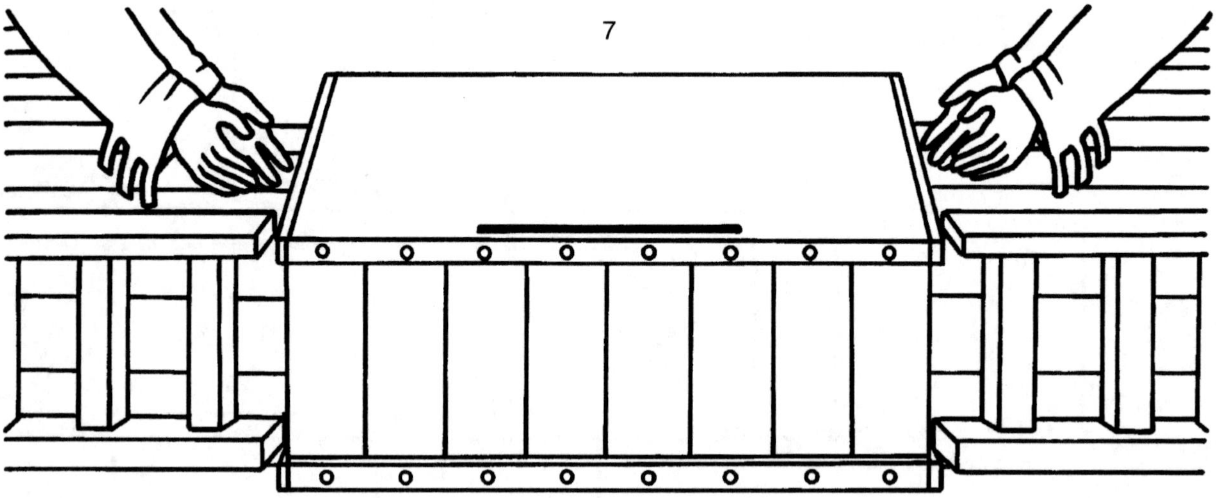

4

The Boston Tea Party

Text for Lift-tabs

The British started taxing the colonists because they were in debt from the French and Indian War. 1

The tax on tea angered the colonists because tea was their favorite drink. 2

Samuel Adams led a group of protestors in Boston. This group, the Sons of Liberty, supported independence from the British. 3

When ships brought a shipment of tea into the Boston harbor, the colonists refused to pay the taxes or to unload the ships. 4

On December 18, 1773, the Sons of Liberty dressed up like Native Americans, went on board the ships, and poured the tea into the harbor. 5

The colonists later called this the Boston Tea Party. 6

The Boston Tea Party was one of many events that led to the Revolutionary War. 7

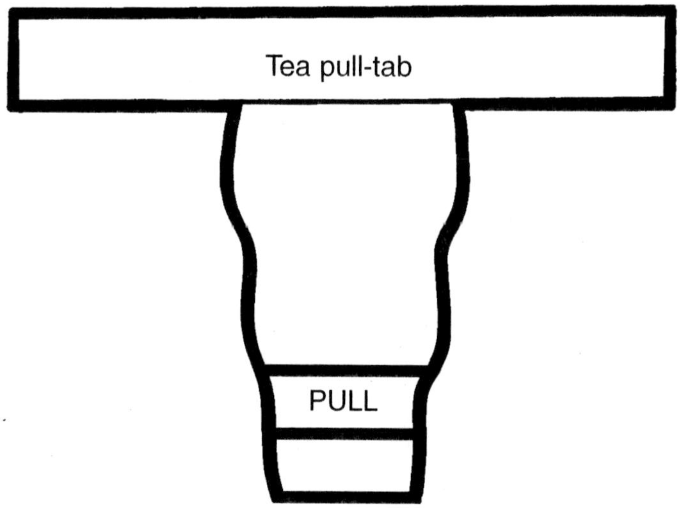

Boston Tea Party Lift-tabs

The Civil Rights Movement

Civil Rights has been an issue for as long as there have been settlers in the United States of America. There are important events which have marked turning points for civil rights among the people of our nation.

Abraham Lincoln wrote the Emancipation Proclamation in 1862 and freed the slaves in 1865 at the end of the Civil War. The freedom that had been longed for for more than 200 years was granted but would take years to be realized.

Almost one hundred years later there was still no real freedom for the African-American. *Segregation*, the act of keeping things or people separated, was practiced in the schools, stores, hotels, restaurants, and restrooms. And even though African-Americans were provided with their own places, they were not equivalent to those designated as "white only."

In the 1950s and 1960s, some radical changes took place that have since improved the quality of life for African-Americans. As a result of the Brown vs. Board of Education suit, a law was passed in 1954 declaring that segregation was unconstitutional. In 1955, Rosa Parks, an African-American seamstress from Alabama, refused to give up her bus seat to a white citizen. She was arrested. The Montgomery Bus Boycott followed, led by the Reverend Martin Luther King, Jr. African-American citizens refused to ride public buses. The boycott lasted nearly a year before the laws were changed allowing paying customers to sit where they wished.

In 1957, a decision to desegregate schools was made in Arkansas but the governor refused to uphold the decision. He ordered the Arkansas National Guard to keep African-Americans out of schools when they opened. President Eisenhower responded by sending 1,000 paratroopers and 10,000 National Guardsmen to overrule the governor. Within a few weeks, the schools were desegregated.

Sit-ins became popular in 1960. The first was held at a Woolworth's in Greensboro, North Carolina. Groups of African-Americans sat at drugstore lunch counters waiting to be served. They took abuse from white citizens and were not served, but they drew attention to the disparity between the way they and white people were treated in restaurants. Freedom Rides were made on buses through towns throughout the country. African-Americans made people everywhere aware of the segregation in bus terminals.

When the first African-American, James Meredith, tried to exercise his right to attend the University of Mississippi, riots broke out and two people died. He graduated from the institution in 1963.

The Civil Rights Movement *(cont.)*

Though the African-American demonstrators were nearly always non-violent, they were often met with violence from police officers as well as citizens. At a 1963 march in Birmingham, Alabama, police even used fire hoses and turned their dogs on the protestors. Many protestors were jailed, including Martin Luther King, Jr. Later that year at the March on Washington, Dr. King made his famous "I Have a Dream" speech. He sought freedom and equal rights for all citizens regardless of race.

In 1965 a march was planned from Selma, Alabama, to Montgomery, Alabama. The protestors wanted to address the governor about the police brutality so many of their people had suffered. The protestors were denied permission to march.

Martin Luther King, Jr., had to appeal to President Johnson to obtain permission. Permission was granted, but some marchers had already begun. They were met with more police brutality. A few weeks later, another march was completed without incident. The Voting Rights Act was passed the same year, allowing persons of any race the right to vote.

Many African-Americans have suffered physical and emotional pain while fighting for Civil Rights. Though there are other Civil Rights issues being addressed all the time, so many strides were made toward fairness during those years. In time, maybe all citizens will enjoy a life where they are treated equally.

 ©Teacher Created Resources, Inc.

The Civil Rights Movement

Map Study

Much of the Civil Rights Movement took place in the South.

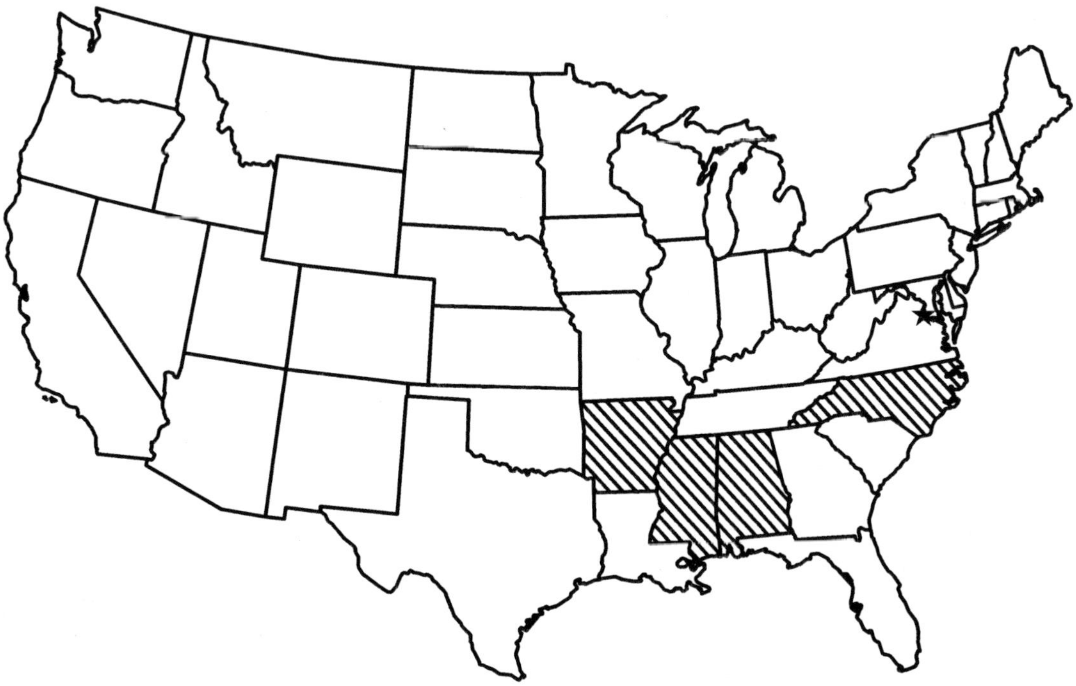

Putting Together
The Civil Rights Movement

Materials

For each student you will need:

- one copy of the text/flap pages (pages 135–137)
- one piece of 12" x 18" construction paper, any color
- scissors
- crayons
- tape or glue

Assembly Directions for the Lift-tab Book

(1) Connect both pages at the tab.

(2) Glue the large, connected page to a piece of construction paper. (The construction paper should form a frame for the page.)

(3) Color the page and the flaps.

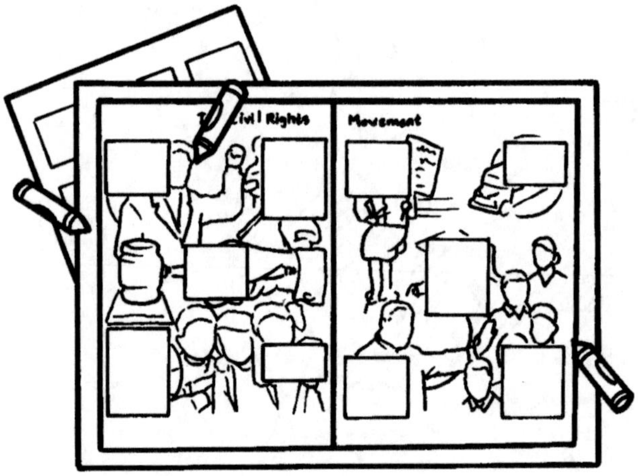

(4) Cut out the flaps. Attach them to the stars above the appropriate text.

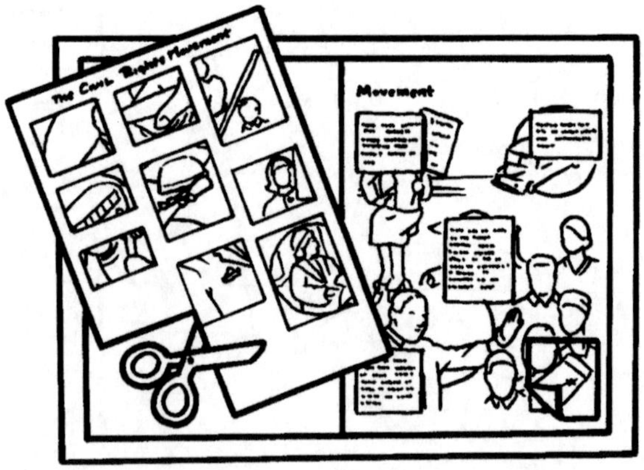

 ©Teacher Created Resources, Inc.

The Civil Rights Movement

Illustration Tabs

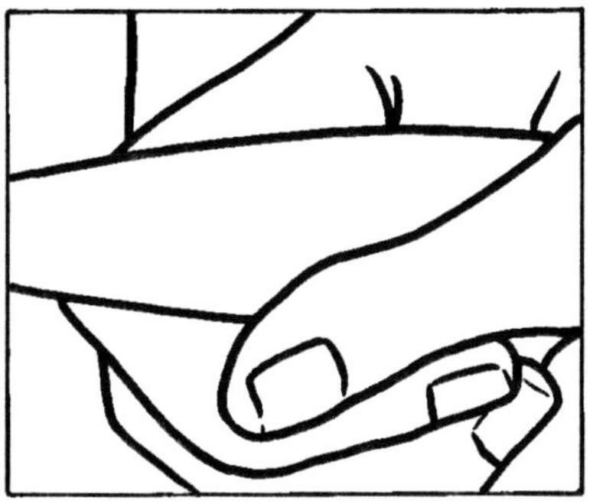

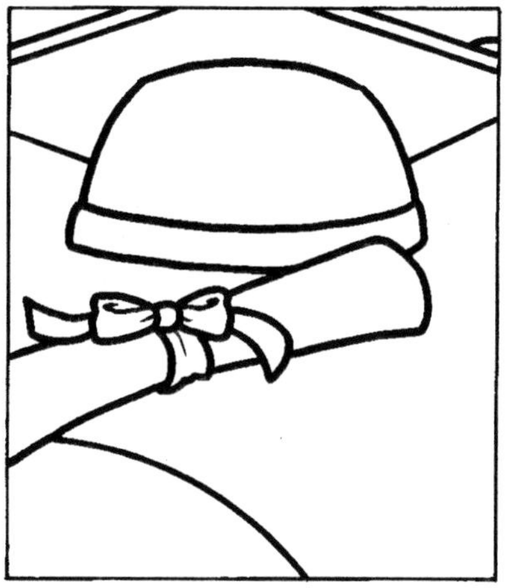

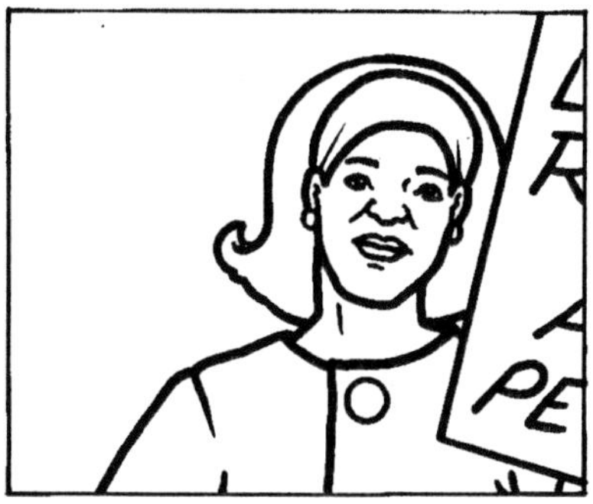

The Civil Rights Movement

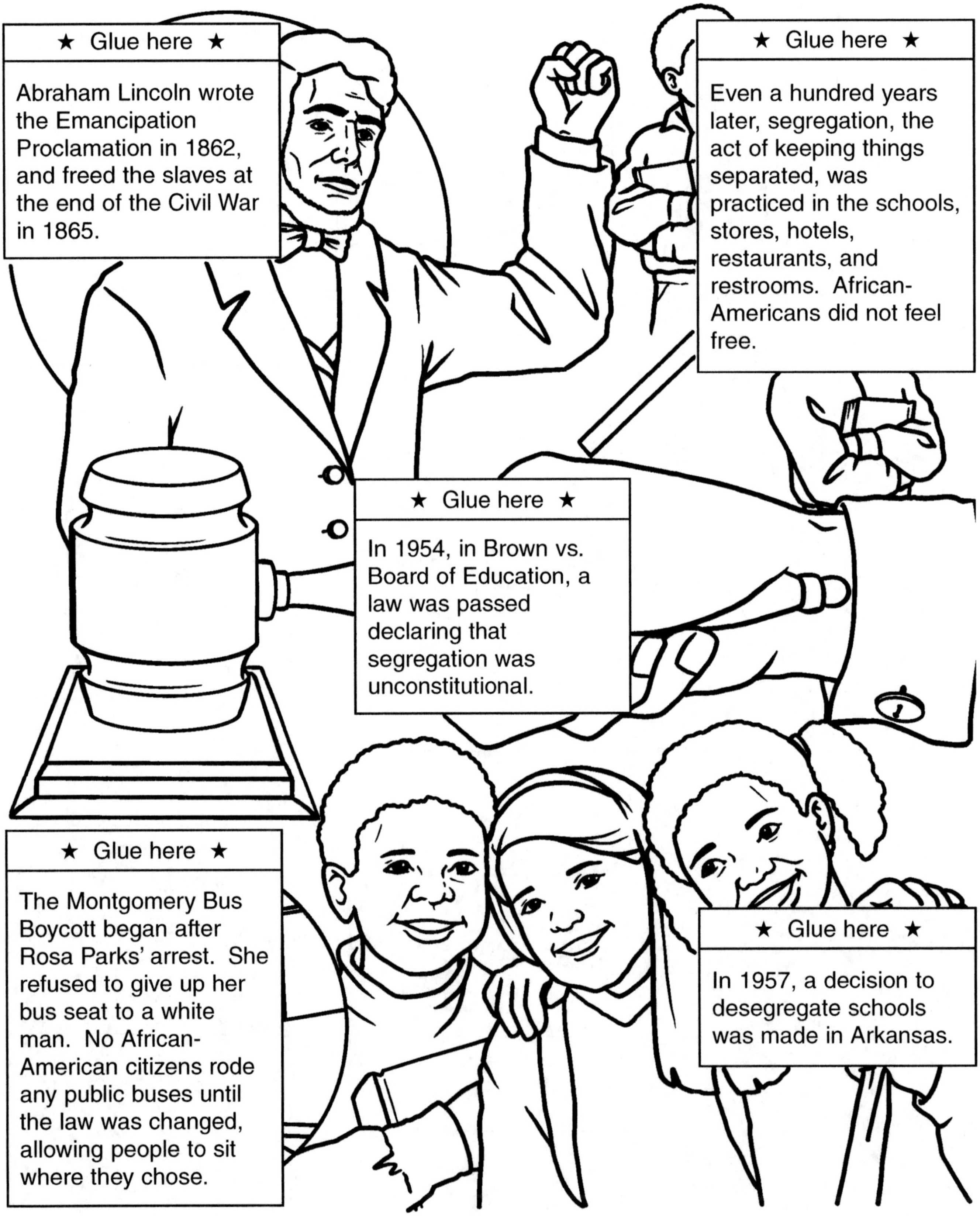

★ Glue here ★

Abraham Lincoln wrote the Emancipation Proclamation in 1862, and freed the slaves at the end of the Civil War in 1865.

★ Glue here ★

Even a hundred years later, segregation, the act of keeping things separated, was practiced in the schools, stores, hotels, restaurants, and restrooms. African-Americans did not feel free.

★ Glue here ★

In 1954, in Brown vs. Board of Education, a law was passed declaring that segregation was unconstitutional.

★ Glue here ★

The Montgomery Bus Boycott began after Rosa Parks' arrest. She refused to give up her bus seat to a white man. No African-American citizens rode any public buses until the law was changed, allowing people to sit where they chose.

★ Glue here ★

In 1957, a decision to desegregate schools was made in Arkansas.

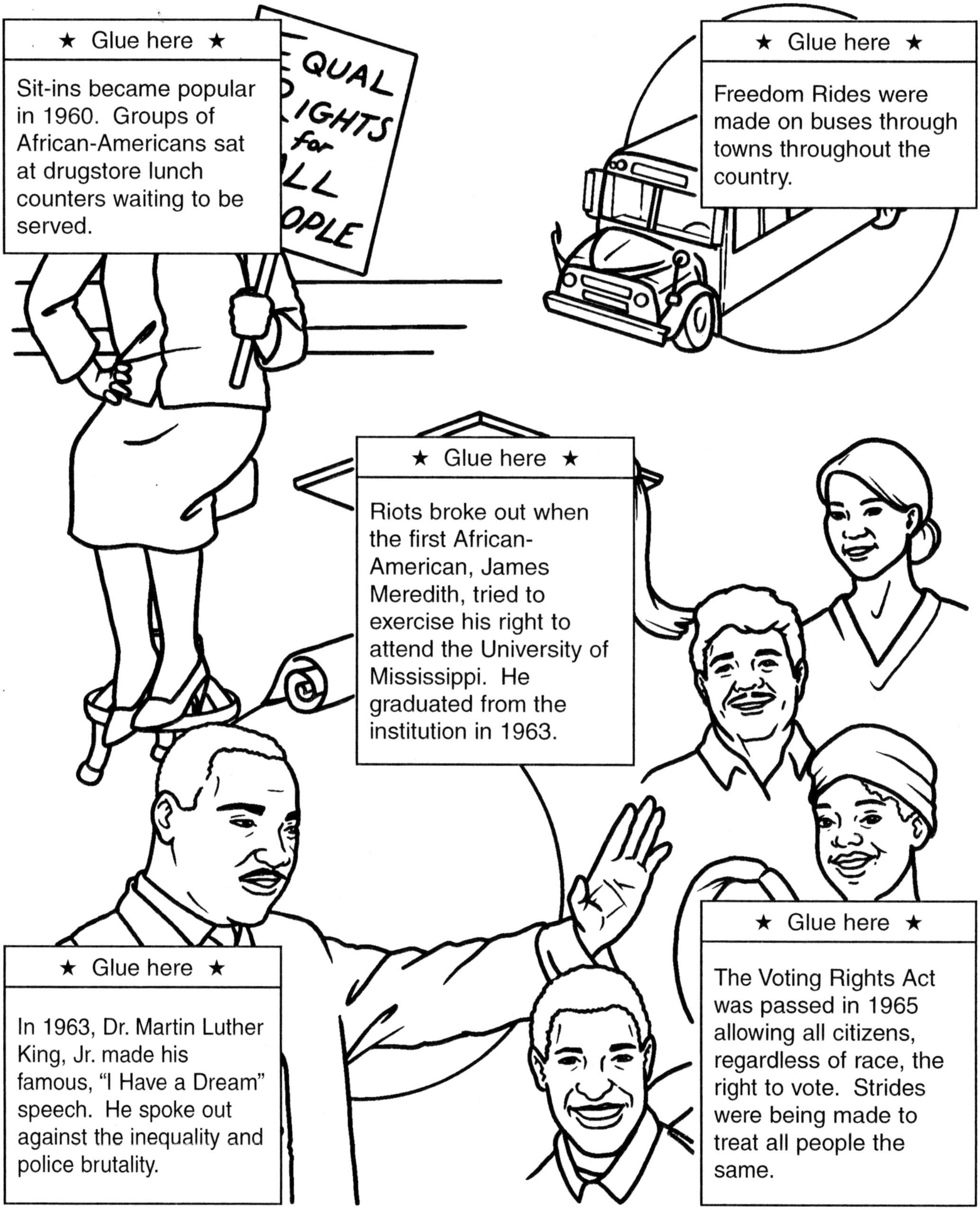

★ Glue here ★

Sit-ins became popular in 1960. Groups of African-Americans sat at drugstore lunch counters waiting to be served.

★ Glue here ★

Freedom Rides were made on buses through towns throughout the country.

★ Glue here ★

Riots broke out when the first African-American, James Meredith, tried to exercise his right to attend the University of Mississippi. He graduated from the institution in 1963.

★ Glue here ★

In 1963, Dr. Martin Luther King, Jr. made his famous, "I Have a Dream" speech. He spoke out against the inequality and police brutality.

★ Glue here ★

The Voting Rights Act was passed in 1965 allowing all citizens, regardless of race, the right to vote. Strides were being made to treat all people the same.

The Oregon Trail

Travel across the west was a trip neither easily made, nor easily forgotten. The destination was Oregon, first named Ouragon by the French in the 1600s. The name means hurricane. It lies on the west side of the Rocky Mountains and joins the Pacific Ocean. Its mystique has held the curiosity of many people on the east coast and for a period of about 30 years enticed more than 300,000 travelers by way of the Oregon Trail.

Robert Stuart, the first person to make the trip, did so in 1812 and 1813. However, he did it coming from the west, from Astoria, to the east. There, a fur company had been established at the mouth of the Columbia River, to St. Louis, where he went to make a progress report.

The first travelers to make the trip from east to west were Jebediah Smith, David E. Jackson, and William Sublette. They went as far as the east side of the Rocky Mountains to take supplies to trappers. The year was 1830.

In 1837, a Scottish explorer hired Alfred J. Miller to accompany him on the trail and paint scenes along the way to show the people back east what the west was like and pique their interest. This coincided nicely with a time when money was tight and success was doubtful in the east. John L. Sullivan wrote in a New York paper that it was “our manifest destiny” to control all of North America. He encouraged people to set out to find their stake.

During the 1840s–1850s, the Oregon Trail was at its most popular. All kinds of people, known as emigrants, headed west. Farmers went for fertile land; fishermen and trappers were attracted by the bounty in the woods and waters; explorers went to make new discoveries; loners went so they could seclude themselves; woodsmen went for good timber; gold prospectors dreamed of becoming wealthy; and some folks just went for the adventure of it.

Covered wagons, called prairie schooners, were the most common mode of transportation. Large groups of about a hundred wagons, a thousand people, and maybe three or four thousand head of cattle traveled together at a speed of about 15 miles per day.

Though many Native Americans were friendly, some could not understand why so many people were coming to claim territory that they felt did not belong to anyone. The emigrants had to learn to protect themselves against various tribes who were sometimes on the attack. However, many lives were lost at the hands of the natives.

Disease, starvation, extreme temperatures, and wild animals also took many lives on the Oregon Trail. About 35,000 people died along the way over the years. Yet, many people did complete the trip and were able to begin a new, prosperous life.

In 1861, the Civil War lured many would-be travelers away from the Oregon Trail to join the armed forces instead. By the time the war was over, railroads and stagecoaches were able to carry west-bound travelers more efficiently. Though there were still a few who traveled on the Oregon Trail, its heyday had come and gone. But for thousands of people the memories were unforgettable.

The Oregon Trail

Map Study

Three hundred thousand people traveled on the Oregon Trail in the mid-1800s.

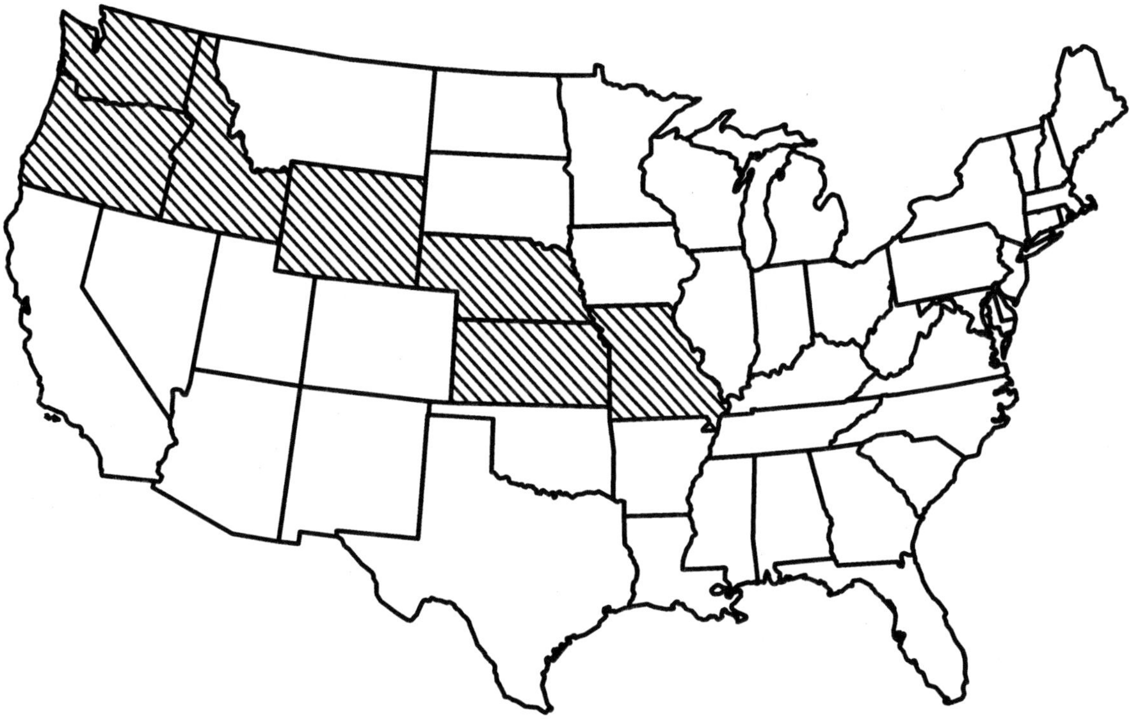

Trace the route taken by settlers traveling on the Oregon Trail. Which states would they have passed through to reach Astoria.

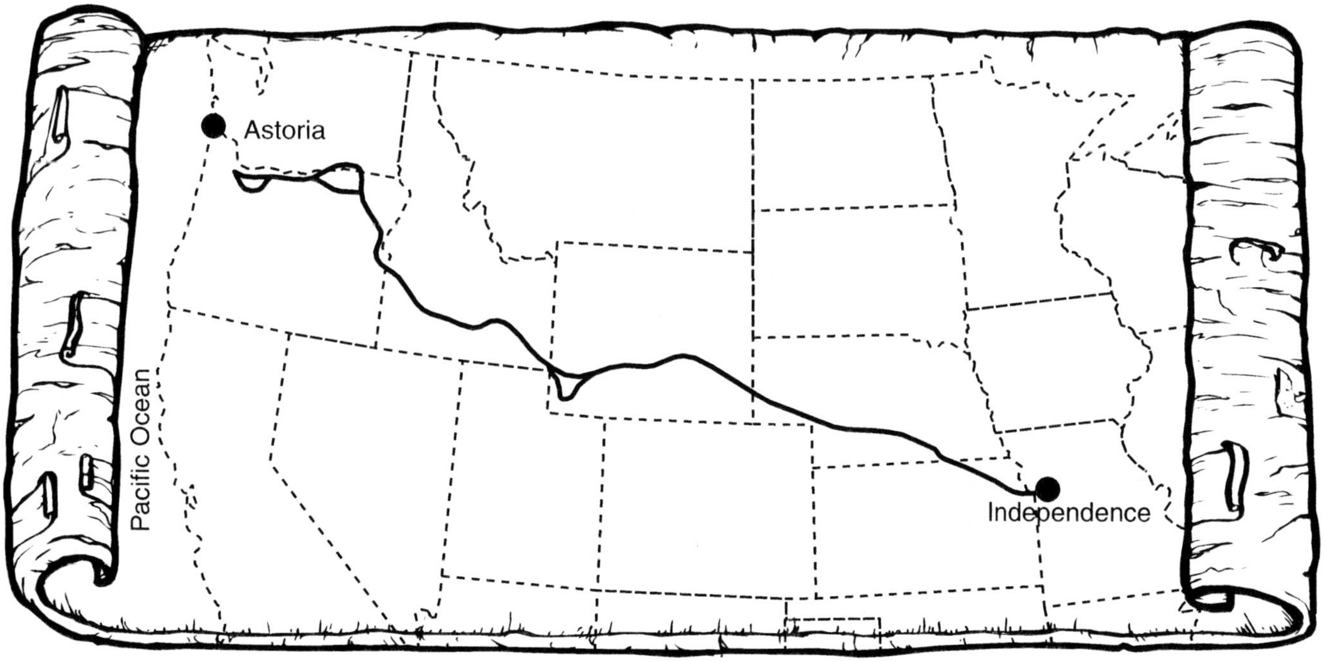

Putting Together *The Oregon Trail*

Materials

For each student you will need:

- one sheet of white paper
- one sheet of brown construction paper
- one sheet of beige construction paper
- one copy of the wagon pattern and text strip (page 141)
- scissors
- glue

Assembly Directions for the Lift-tab Book

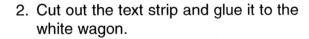

1. Run off one copy of the pattern on white paper and another on brown construction paper. Cut out each pattern.
2. Cut out the text strip and glue it to the white wagon.
3. Place the brown wagon directly on top of the white wagon and staple them together across the top, creating the lift tab.
4. Glue one short end of the beige paper on top of the staples.
5. Curve the beige paper to the back of the wagon, being sure not to crease (fold) it. Glue other end to the back of the wagon, creating the wagon cover.

 ©Teacher Created Resources, Inc.

The Oregon Trail

Wagon Pattern

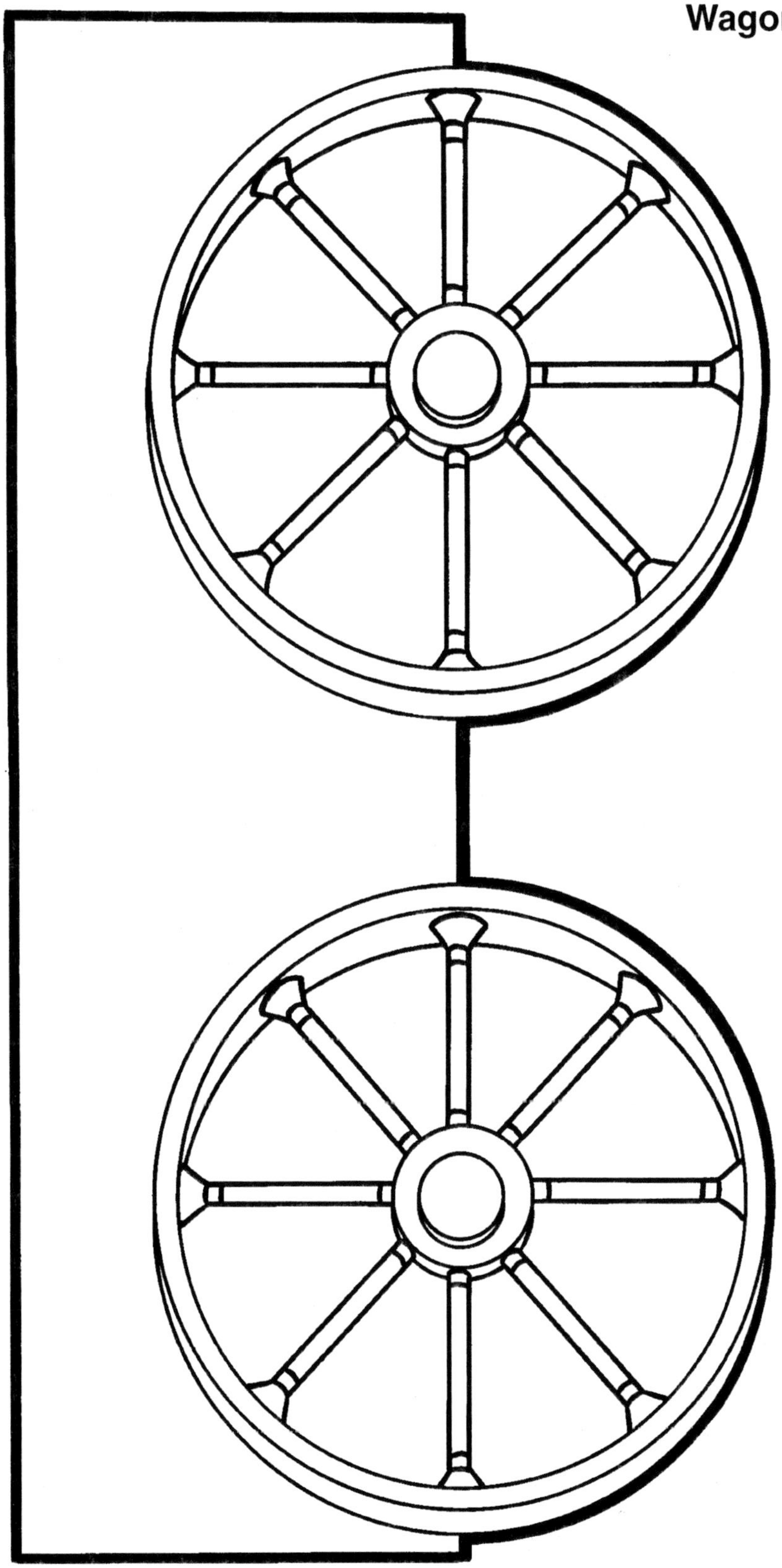

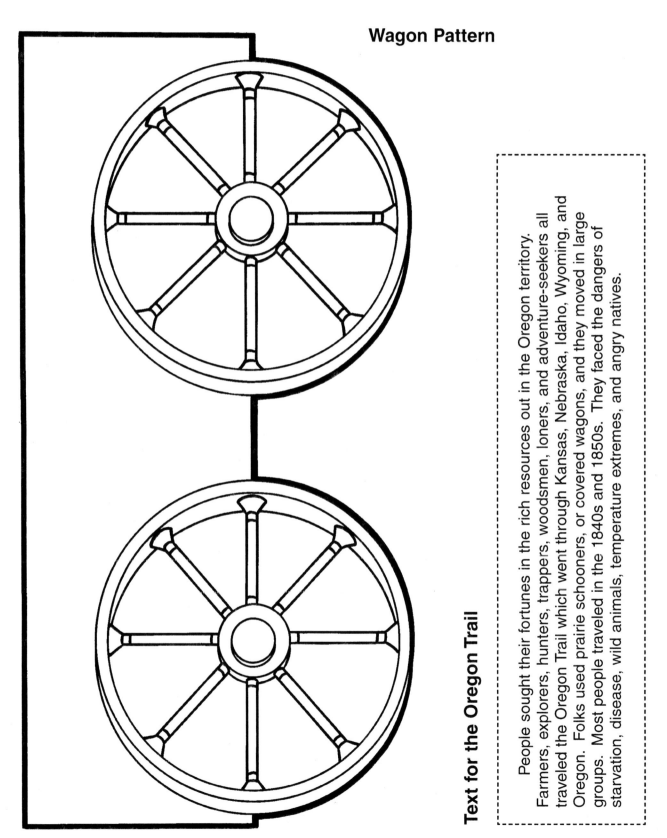

Text for the Oregon Trail

People sought their fortunes in the rich resources out in the Oregon territory. Farmers, explorers, hunters, trappers, woodsmen, loners, and adventure-seekers all traveled the Oregon Trail which went through Kansas, Nebraska, Idaho, Wyoming, and Oregon. Folks used prairie schooners, or covered wagons, and they moved in large groups. Most people traveled in the 1840s and 1850s. They faced the dangers of starvation, disease, wild animals, temperature extremes, and angry natives.

Map of the United States

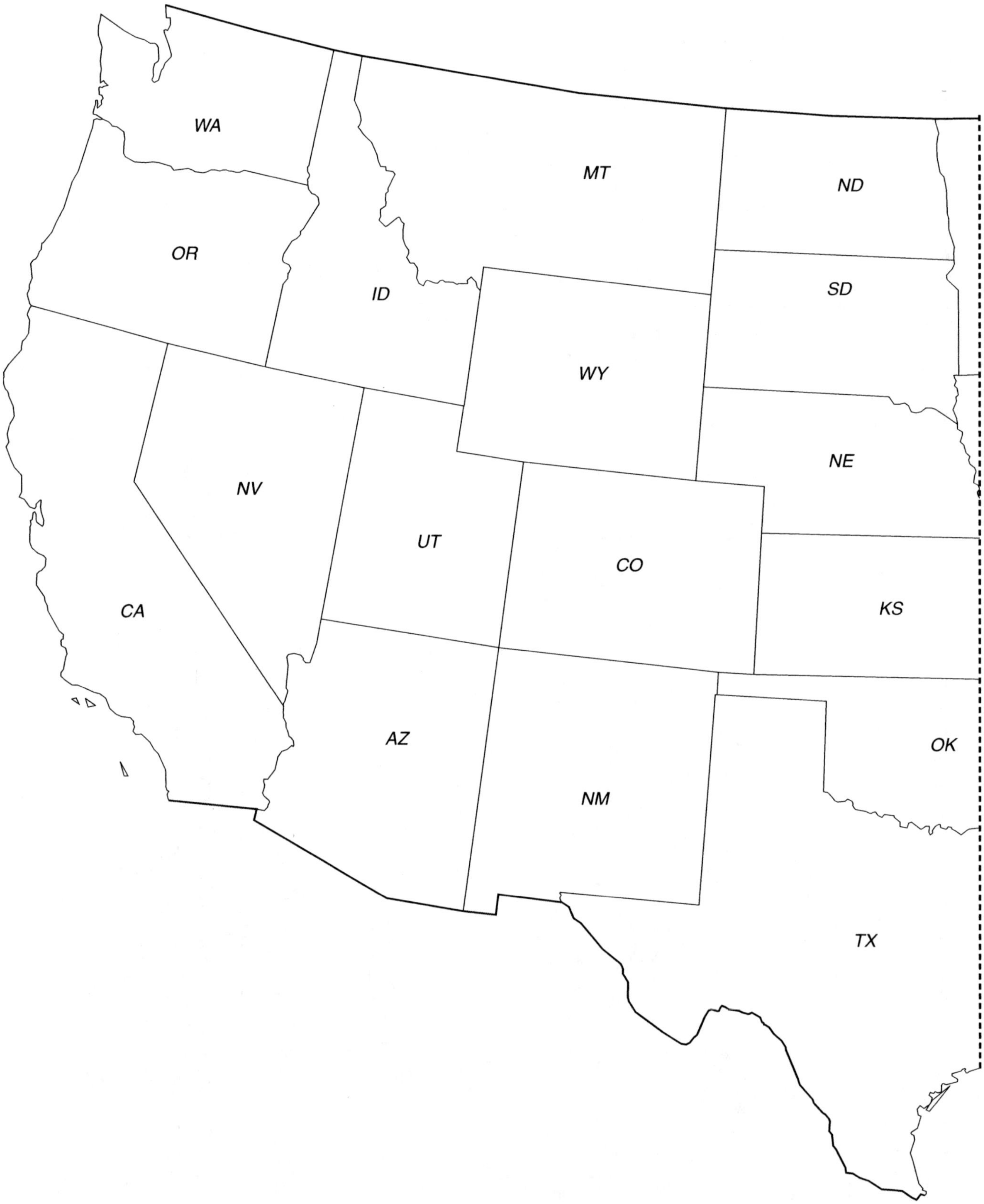

Map of the United States *(cont.)*

Map of the United States *(cont.)*

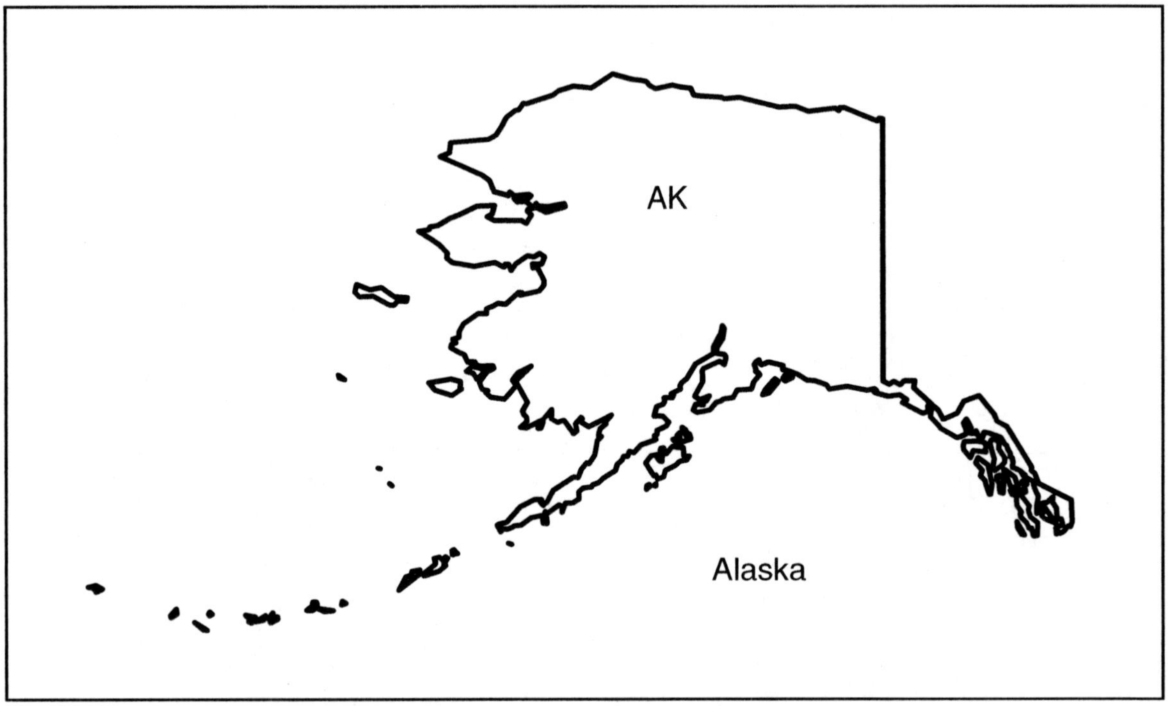

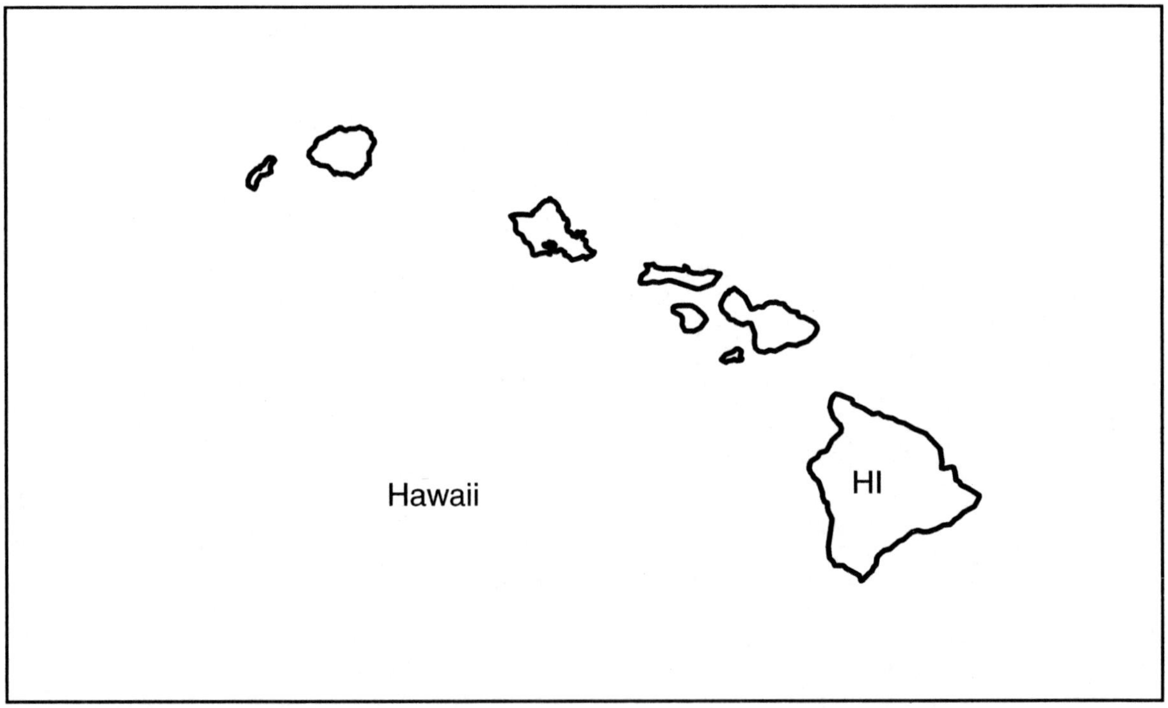